License to Dream: Every Woman's Guide to Financial Freedom Through Network Marketing, ©2010 Judy O'Higgins, Kristi Lee, Karen Palmer. Published and distributed in the United States by Eagle One Publishing, LLC, www.eagleonepublishing.com. Publisher: Melody Marler Forshee, Eagle One Publishing, LLC. Cover design by Dave Baker, The Baker Group. Photography by Rafy Ruiz, Hayuya Pictures.

For information about special discounts for bulk purchases, contact Eagle One Publishing, info@eagleonepublishing.com.

ISBN: 978-1-936677-10-8

Printed in the United States of America

The hypothetical examples set forth in this book are intended to explain elements of network marketing. These hypotheticals are not representative of the income, if any, that an independent distributor can or will earn, and any figures used are not a representation of earnings you should anticipate. Similarly, any downline growth examples presented shows a downline organization growing in symmetrical fashion. This is for purposes of illustration only; in reality, organizations do not grow fully or symmetrically. Success with a network marketing business results only from successful sales efforts, which require effort, diligence, and leadership. Your success will depend upon how effectively you exercise these qualities.

EAGLE ONE
PUBLISHING

To Kody Bateman, thank you for dreaming big and never giving up on your dreams. We share the same dream of changing the world. You gave me the vehicle to do it, and my life will never be the same.

Judy O'Higgins

To God, thank you for putting a huge vision in my heart and giving me the gifts and talents to inspire people. To my daughter, Jade, you are my biggest "why" and I am incredibly blessed to be your mom. To my mother, Rose, thank you for your unwavering support and your belief that I can achieve anything. To my BCM, thank you for always walking through fire with me and having enough faith for both of us when I needed it. To women everywhere, may you be true to yourself and have the courage to step into your greatness...together we can change the world.

Kristi Lee

To my family whose love and support I know I can always count on...may you always have the courage to dream big!

Karen Palmer

Contents

If you are a woman considering starting a network marketing business or newly involved in one, this could be one of the most important books you will read. The authors speak to women entrepreneurs of every age group with the authority that comes from experience, and provide a vehicle that could help anyone achieve a breakthrough in their network marketing business. If you follow the process outlined in *License to Dream* you can expect life-changing results. You will be inspired to dream big, set goals and follow the systematic steps to success outlined in the book.

Eric Lofholm
Eric Lofholm International

The three road warriors, Judy, Kristi and Karen, have put together an easy-to-use guide that's packed full of valuable, hands-on information. This is a "must-read" for every woman looking for financial freedom. Your potential after reading it is limitless!

Susan Friedmann, CSP
bestselling author, *Riches in Niches:
How to Make it BIG in a small Market*

If you've ever wondered how you are going to create the financial freedom you desire, you've now got the vehicle, the map, and the key to your dreams. It doesn't get any clearer than laid out in *License to Dream*.

Jan Janzen
Bestselling author

Women are naturally much better networkers than men. Here is a great book that helps not only with the step-by-step approach to our business, but also gives the big picture. It's great to have them both in one place, with an easy-to-read book.

Tom "Big Al" Schreiter
BigAlreport.com

Judy O'Higgins, Kristi Lee, and Karen Palmer have written a book that combines wisdom with practicality, and loftiness with down-to-earth lessons that can be practiced on a daily basis. Other books have been written for women in network marketing, but few if any achieve that ultimate benchmark that all authors strive for: The information is grounded enough, and profound enough that, when implemented, can assure the reader she will go to higher ground. The authors borrow from their combined experience, which makes this a powerhouse of a book because of its authenticity. *License to Dream* is a book that you will want to read, savor, and share with everyone who longs for freedom.

Rosie Bank
Author, *You, Inc.: Own Your Business, Own Your Life*

Brilliant and full of wisdom! This book is your map to success as a woman in network marketing! I love the "key facts" and the real stories of women who are walking the walk. Bravo!

Diane Cunningham
Founder and president, National Association of
Christian Women Entrepreneurs

Introduction
OUR DREAMS

Do you remember the dreams you had as a little girl? Did you want to be a lawyer? A teacher? A CEO? A mom? An astronaut? An author? A movie star? As a child, we believe we can do and be anything. But, somewhere along the way, we seem to lose that wonder of childhood. We forget what it means to dream big—or to dream at all.

Do you find yourself lying awake in bed worrying about losing your job? Have you already lost your job and searched in vain for a new one? Are you wishing that you could find a way to create a better future for yourself and your family? Instead of dreaming, are you worrying?

Maybe you are a Baby Boomer facing a big crack in your retirement nest egg with shrinking 401(k)s, frozen pensions, and reduced home values. With the average 401(k) balance falling 27 percent and over $2 trillion lost—so far—millions of Baby Boomers are postponing retirement because they are afraid they can't afford to stop working. Is this you?

Maybe you are still young, but stressed out and working insane hours at your job. Are you depressed over being unable to spend quality time with your spouse and children and feel the pain of missing out on the important events in your children's lives?

- Have you lost your dreams for your future or see them fading away?
- Are you willing to think outside the box to get your dreams back?
- Are you ready for a change?

If you answered, "Yes," you have come to the right place! Our goal for this book is to give you back your life's dreams and provide the tools to make them come true.

It's time to stop waiting to retire, to stop waiting until your kids grow up, and to stop waiting to get out of debt. It's time to stop putting the true desires of your heart on hold. Our desire is to empower you to recapture your dreams and, more than that, to pursue and manifest them. Not later...now!

WHO ARE WE?

We are three women representing diverse age groups, from Baby Boomer to young stay-at-home mom, who made a decision NOT to place our lives on hold any longer. Through the magic of network marketing, we are moving toward the freedom we've always dreamed of—that all of us dream of. Although we are in different stages of life and in different stages of our journey toward financial freedom, we have all given ourselves a license to dream big—to allow ourselves to conceive of the formerly impossible as possible.

In this book, we'll show you how we are achieving our dreams by thinking "outside the box" and using a simple concept to create financial freedom, time freedom, and lifestyle freedom. Here is a snapshot of the freedoms we have achieved and want to help you reach too.

JUDY *(Retired Baby Boomer)*

Judy wakes up when she wants to, plays with her dog Baxter, and takes the 30-second commute to her home office in her pajamas. She works when she chooses and has no boss telling her when to go to lunch. She never has to ask for a vacation—she just books a flight and hops on a plane.

Judy is her own boss and has total control over her choices. She can go meet a friend for coffee any day of the week, catch a movie matinee, or take a cruise to Alaska at a moment's notice. She hasn't had to live by a 9-to-5 routine in years. After just two years with her home-based business, she matched her income from her 25-year career as a counselor and retired!

Judy receives checks in the mail automatically every week—some with commas in them (for example: $1,000 or more!) Her retirement is funded for the rest of her life—regardless of what happens to the stock market, Social Security, or the economy. She sleeps like a baby every night, knowing that these checks will keep coming in forever and her retirement is secure. She is grateful every day for the blessing of financial security and knowing she will never have to get a part time job to help with the mortgage or pay her bills.

KRISTI *(Corporate America Survivor)*

Kristi is able to set her own schedule each day since she left corporate America. She is able to go on every school field trip with her daughter, volunteer in her daughter's classroom, and spearhead projects like raising thousands of dollars for her daughter's Girl Scout troop selling Girl Scout cookies without worrying about it interfering with a job. She attends seminars and events without having to ask a boss for permission. She will never have to be told to relocate her family one more time since resigning from the corporate rat race and becoming her own boss with her own home-based business.

Now Kristi can put her training and marketing talents to work for herself and her own business team, instead of making someone else in corporate America wealthy. She sets her own business schedule, works the hours she chooses, and feels grateful for the freedom and security of being in control of her own life. She is on her way to financial freedom and lifestyle freedom!

KAREN *(Stay-at-home mom)*

Karen, a mom with three children, chooses her projects and her deadlines. When it rains outside, she can take time with her kids to bake chocolate chip cookies and make hot cocoa. On a sunny afternoon, she and her kids take time off to run in the sprinklers and eat Popsicles. She can pack up a picnic lunch and head to the park any day, or every day! Her time is her own, and she chooses to spend it putting her family first.

As a college professor, Karen had to schedule her family around her job. With her business, she schedules her job around her family. She and her husband take time to play with their kids. When they go on business trips, they make it a family vacation. They get out of their home-based business what they put in, and that time and effort is leveraged as their business grows. They are looking forward to a life of complete financial freedom—no debt, no worries about paying bills on time or using the credit card to buy groceries, no fear of losing their home.

Even though each of us has a different lifestyle, we each receive checks in the mail regularly, which allows us time and lifestyle freedom. How did we achieve this? How can YOU? The answer is residual income.

This book is a roadmap that guides you step-by-step through how to achieve the same results. We invite you to leave behind your self-doubt, skepticism, and "old thinking." Pick up the roadmap in this book, follow the steps we have laid out for you in the following chapters, and give yourself a license to dream again. Join us and thousands of others on the road to financial freedom. It's all here for you if you are ready!

KEY POINT

NOTE: We have used an analogy of driving a car and taking a trip to describe what it is like for a woman who is unfamiliar with network marketing to come away with a better understanding, not only about the industry, but also herself. Throughout the book you will find "key facts" (denoted with the "Key Point" graphic like the one shown here) that we believe are significant in building a successful business. These facts have helped us shorten our learning curve and increase our earning curve!

Cherish your visions and your dreams, as they are the children of your soul, the blueprints of your ultimate achievements.

—NAPOLEON HILL

CHAPTER 1

The Super Highway to Financial Freedom

If you're like most women, you've probably spent a lot of time thinking about what would need to happen for you to achieve your dreams. Have you fantasized about winning the lottery? Getting a surprise inheritance? Marrying rich? There's a better way—because it's totally within your control. What if there was a way to get paid over and over again, just for telling people about an amazing product or service that you already use and love?

THE MAGIC OF RESIDUAL INCOME

If you are new to the concept and the power of residual income, here's a brief explanation. Most of us are familiar with the idea that, once a song is recorded, the artist gets a small amount of money every time that song airs on radio or TV and every time someone buys her CD or otherwise accesses her music. An artist can record a song once and receive ongoing royalty income from many people listening to it for years to come. THAT is residual income—and it's why Elvis makes more money now than when he was alive!

Here's another example. When you buy a book on amazon.com, the author receives a small amount of money for that sale. It's not much by itself. The power is in many people buying it over time, creating a monthly revenue stream for the author for something she did one time (writing the book).

THAT is residual income.

If you're not a gifted writer or singer, you can still create this kind of ongoing income and benefit from receiving checks every month for life. We know because we have done it, and SO CAN YOU! Here's how.

Have you ever gone to a great movie or a restaurant that you loved and then told your family, co-workers, and friends about it? What if you got a check in the mail every time one of those people (which we call your "network") went to the movie or ate in the restaurant? What if you recommended that movie or restaurant to 50 people, and 40 of them went? If your recommendation or referral bonus was $10 per person, you would receive checks totaling $400 just for telling people you know about the movie and restaurant. If you did the same thing the next month, you would receive another check for $400. What could you do with an extra $400 a month?

NETWORK MARKETING

In today's world, the typical consumer is overly bombarded with advertising on TV, radio, the internet, print media—even cell phones! Traditional advertising and marketing has become less and less effective in this information age because we have learned to tune it out just to survive.

However, the "old-fashioned" concept of one person recommending a product or service they love to others is alive and well, and the personal recommendation is even MORE powerful in today's society where impersonal technology rules, because it came from a trusted source.

Many companies have come to this conclusion and are using an alternative business model called "network marketing" to get the word out about their products and services. There are thousands of companies using the network marketing model today because "word of mouth" advertising is more effective than ever.

The basis of this model is the simple concept that if someone loves a product or service and tells others about it, she deserves to be financially rewarded by the company that makes the product or provides the service when her "referrals" purchase it.

Have you ever caught yourself saying, "I wish I had a dollar for every time I told someone about _____"? Well, now you can, and those dollars can add up fast!

Going back to the example of getting paid for recommending a movie or restaurant: What if you got paid AGAIN every time those 40 people went back to eat at that restaurant for life?

THAT is residual income—getting paid over and over for something you did one time! And that is how Judy got to retire, Kristi got to leave corporate America, and Karen gets to stay home with her kids.

MORE MAGIC: LEVERAGED INCOME

Let's take our example one step further. What if you got paid AGAIN when the people who ate in the restaurant you recommended told THEIR friends, family, and co-workers, who also tried the restaurant? How about getting paid yet AGAIN when those people tell THEIR network of friends, family, and associates, who also then visit the restaurant? And then AGAIN when this group repeats the process?

Repeat this scenario several more times—now you can imagine how you could receive substantial income for something you started, but which then took on a life of its own without you—and get paid over and over and over every time someone buys a product or service that you or someone in your network recommends!

There are many thousands of people successfully doing just that to pay their mortgages, finance their retirements, raise their families, send their children to college, and escape the corporate rat race. Thousands of ordinary women (like the three of us), with no special education or previous skills, are creating the kind of income that can bring their dreams back to life and sustain them with a lifestyle many would not believe possible. If you want to be one of them, this book will show you how we are doing it and what you need to do to get the same results.

THE BUSINESS MODEL FOR TODAY'S ECONOMY

Robert Kiyosaki is one of the most respected and successful business writers and entrepreneurs of our time. His newest book, *The Business of the 21st Century*, heartily endorses network marketing as the best business model for the average woman to create her own wealth in today's economy.

He correctly points out that the old success model of getting a good job and sticking with it for years is over. Job security, retirement pensions, savings, and the 401k are pretty much gone. An expensive college education no longer is a guarantee of a good job. With bad news of unemployment, bankruptcies, foreclosures, and a loss of retirement assets hitting us daily, Kiyosaki urges us to let go of our old ideas about how to build economic security for our families and embrace the new models for achieving our dreams. He urges us all to take control of our financial destinies by becoming entrepreneurs, and he recommends network marketing as the absolute best way for the average person to do just that!

For those who want to follow his advice, the time is **now** to start a business that can take you down the road to financial freedom, lifestyle freedom, and **true** security for yourself and your family. Network marketing is truly the best business model for today's economy.

TOP 10 BENEFITS OF NETWORK MARKETING

Below is a summary of the many benefits of network marketing that make it what we believe to be the best choice for you if you don't want to keep trading time for money in your job, don't want to keep working forever, and don't want the headaches and financial risk of a traditional business or franchise.

1) You're the boss

When you decide to share a company's products or services for profit, you are an independent contractor, NOT an employee. This means you have no boss, no supervisor, no one to answer to but yourself. You do get guidance and help from the company as well as from the person who introduced you to the company and the product ideas, but without the downside of having to report to a boss as in the traditional business model. **You** are truly your own boss and in charge of your financial destiny.

2) Forget the 9-to-5 routine

You can focus as few or as many hours each week as you choose to put into your home business, and you choose which hours. You also have no employees to manage, like you would in a franchise model or traditional business. You have total freedom to run your business in the way that works best for your lifestyle. Most people in network marketing work only part-time, yet it is possible to replace your full-time job income in just a few years of part-time effort with the network marketing model. The flexibility of working hours is also a great benefit to women who choose to stay at home with their children—imagine working your home business around your children's naptime like Karen does.

3) No commute to an office

You can operate out of your home office or from your dining room table. With the current fluctuation in gas prices, the commute from your bedroom to your home office is a huge benefit. Most of us just need a phone, computer, and high-speed internet access, and we're all set. The simplicity of the network marketing business model is a benefit that cannot be overemphasized.

4) Reduce your taxes

With a home business, you can write off the cost of a phone, computer, and high speed internet, among other things. You can also get reimbursed for every mile you drive that you can relate to your home business (50 cents per mile in 2010). Other deductions may include a percentage of your utility bills (depending on what percentage of your home is taken up by your home office), uninsured health care expenses, equipment such as a camera, computer, printer, and more (consult your accountant or financial advisor). The tax breaks for home-based businesses are some of the **best** in America today, and this alone can save the average taxpayer thousands a year. Would you rather have the taxes taken out of what you earn first and live on what's left, like most people do, or earn money, live, and pay taxes on what's left, like we do?

5) Low start-up cost

There are well over 1,000 companies today using the network marketing business model to spread the word about their products. Why? Because it works. Word-of-mouth recommendation for a product or service is much more powerful than advertising. In most cases, the start-up cost to get your business going ranges from only $25 to $500. Even on the high end, a person can get started for under $1,000. Contrast that with the franchise and traditional business models where start-up costs typically run many thousands of dollars, and you can see one big reason why this type of business is so attractive, especially in our current economy. The risk and upfront investment are minimal. And don't forget that, unlike the others, this type of business can be worked part-time around your lifestyle, or full-time for faster results. Either way, it beats shelling out $50,000 to $200,000 or more for a franchise or traditional business, assuming you could get a loan for one in today's economy!

6) High reward potential

The network marketing model offers average people the chance to make excellent income with no limits imposed by a corporate salary structure. There is also no glass ceiling to limit the advancement of women. Everyone starts with a level playing field and has the same potential for success. Promotions are based solely on your efforts, not the whims of your boss. Remember that in the franchise and traditional business models, it typically takes years to break even before you see a profit. With the network marketing model, you can be profitable after just a few weeks—and go on to replace your job income and beyond to achieve your financial goals and dreams. There are no limits here to what can be achieved!

7) Receive checks with commas—residual income

After a relatively short time (usually months, not years) of consistent work with a network marketing business, entrepreneurs can be receiving regular monthly checks with commas in them! Doesn't that beat the heck out of waiting for your monthly Social Security check that barely pays your grocery bills, or worrying about how much less your home is worth this month than 12 months ago, or if your job will still be there next week?

As long as your product users keep buying and using the product you recommended, you will continue to receive these checks automatically, like the singer who continues to get royalty checks from songs they recorded years ago. This ability to receive monthly residual income over and over from a sale you made one time is a key component of what truly sets network marketing apart from other business models.

After a few years of building up this type of business, you can do whatever you want, like take a world cruise or travel the country and, should you become ill, the monthly checks just keep coming in like clockwork! This is the meaning of TRUE financial security and freedom—not being dependent on corporate America, the government, or any other entity for your financial health.

8) Leverage yourself

All the financial experts from Donald Trump to Robert Kiyosaki say you must leverage yourself to create true wealth, and the network marketing model does just that. Here's how it works:

- You find a product you love and start using it.
- You recommend it to a few others who also start using it. You get paid for each one.
- Some of them also want an income from recommending the product to others they know. You get paid a coaching bonus for each one who follows your lead and duplicates what you are doing, plus you earn a percentage of everything they and **their** customers buy every month.
- This repetition continues down a line of people for several levels through the process of duplication, and your checks start growing. You are getting paid on everything that is being transacted by your team, as well as on your own efforts.
- Your team grows and you start getting checks for what the newer people on it are doing—and you may not even know them. Your team expands to several states, eventually all of them, and your checks go up every month!

9) No more trading time for dollars

In the "job world," you can only work so many hours, and your income is limited by that reality. Even a second job only adds so much, and then you are at your limit. In the network marketing world, the hours you spend can be duplicated by your team. If you work five hours a week in your home business and you have ten people on your team each also working five hours, that is 50 hours of productivity in a week—plus your five hours. Can your job do that?

10) Personal growth

Network marketing has been described as a personal growth program with a compensation plan attached. You will be learning new skills. You will surround yourself with positive messages and people. To be successful, you will focus on creating and maintaining a positive attitude and mindset. In a world where everything we hear is 87 percent negative, you will become a beacon of hope to those who come into your business and into your life. You will ultimately help many others improve their lives as well.

Does all of this sound too good to be true? Trust us, it's not. People all over the world are using the magic of network marketing to enable them to dream again. We are doing it, and so can you. And there has never been a better time than right now—today!

THINK IT OVER:

What are some of the dreams you have put aside?

How could network marketing and residual income help you get them back?

What are you most excited about after reading this chapter?

What questions do you still have?

CHAPTER 2

Choose Your Vehicle

If you have made the decision to join us on the road trip to financial freedom with network marketing and get that residual income stream started—congratulations! Before you jump in with both feet, here is a tip that can keep you motivated as you build your business, while others fail before they get started.

BELIEVE IN YOUR PRODUCT & COMPANY

Your network marketing "career" will likely require three to five years of working part-time to replace your job income (Judy did it in two) and an estimated five to ten years total to achieve true financial freedom and generational wealth, depending on how fast you choose to go. Since you will be sharing a product or service for that length of time to build up the income of your dreams, it is CRITICAL that you really love and believe in your product and its value. If not, you will lack the passion for it that attracts others to you like a magnet.

Here's the key: Would you use, love and recommend the product(s) to others whether or not you were getting paid?

If the answer is "no," then do not sign up with that company! The importance of this cannot be overstated. Many people get started with the first company they hear about, instead of doing their homework and choosing a product/service that they truly feel passionate about. If you pick a company randomly and are only doing it for the money, your road could be long and bumpy.

THE PRODUCT

If you know and believe in your heart that your product/service can absolutely benefit every person's life with whom you share it, your path will be much easier; you will achieve your goals and dreams more quickly because of the positive energy you send out to the world and your passion for helping others with the product. So choose wisely!

Here are some practical questions to ask yourself when considering the types of products to choose from:

1)   Is something similar in quality or price offered in stores like Walgreens, Target, or WalMart? If so, be prepared to compete with those types of retail stores if your potential product line includes widely distributed products.

2)   Are there other network marketing companies offering a similar product or service? Remember, your potential customer can be confused by several people telling them, "Ours is the best."

3) The ideal product/service to align yourself with:
 • Has little or no competition or stands out from the crowd.
 • Is not subject to whims of government regulatory groups like the FDA or FTC.
 • Is easy to use.
 • Solves a common problem.
 • Has potential for high physical or emotional positive impact.

4) What is the model the company uses for sharing its products? Does that model fit with your personality and lifestyle?

If you love cosmetics, skin care, jewelry, or women's clothing and love to entertain, your ideal company could be one that sells these products and uses the "home party" model to spread the word.

If you are a technology buff, pick a company that will have you representing a new high tech product or service that could be shared over the Internet.

Do you love to cook? There are companies that will pay you for demonstrating and recommending cookware and kitchen products.

If you are passionate about healthy living and want to grow your income by helping others become healthier, consider the companies that feature vitamins, air and water filters, weight loss, and other health-oriented products.

If you would prefer a "product" that is a service so you don't have to deal with inventory, returns, and cost of samples and shipping, consider companies that offer legal services, communications, or Internet-based greeting cards.

5) What are the distributor purchasing requirements? All companies using the network marketing model ask that their representatives buy and use their product/service themselves. After all, how can you recommend something you have no personal experience with? This is another important reason to LOVE your product/service, as you will be a "product of your product" for your career with the company. The good news is you will always get the discounted/lowest price as long as you order every month. (There can be a wide variation in the monthly cost, however, depending on how expensive your product/service is. Some are as low as $30 per month, while others cost well in excess of $100 per month.) Again, do your homework and ask questions to gain awareness of your potential company's requirements before you join them as an independent representative.

THE COMPANY

After you have chosen the type of product or service, the next important step is to evaluate the company itself and especially the leadership. You can have the world's greatest product, but if the company is mismanaged or the leadership is not sharp, passionate about their product, and in it for the long term, or if they do not understand how to work with the network marketing model, the company will likely not last.

Do some research on your potential choice. Meet the founders and CEO if you can; otherwise, get on a conference call they host. Pay close attention to the energy they bring to the call or personal meeting, as well as their words.

• Do they have a big vision for the company?

- What is the "culture" or philosophy of the company?
- Are they passionate about their product?
- Do they put the needs of their independent representatives at the top of their priority list? Do they have shareholders to answer to? (Remember–their decisions will directly affect you.)
- Do they have a solid and well-conceived plan for the company's future growth?
- Find out about the company's debt situation.
- If you can, tour the home office to see how the product is made. Is it elaborate and expensive to produce? (The higher the cost of creating the products, the more expensive and less competitive they will be.)
- Meet the home office employees or listen to how the customer service reps sound on the phone. Do they seem happy and eager to be helpful? Is it a hassle to get through to customer service or a pleasant experience? Remember, these folks will be your future customer service reps, handling the people you refer to buy your product/service.

THE BOTTOM LINE

You want a CEO and leadership team who are totally committed to the company long-term and who have a personal passion for what the product/service can do to help people. The CEO is not just there for the adventure of starting and growing a company and then selling it. He/she has a big vision and dreams of making a difference.

Your future success in network marketing depends on a company whose leaders have the heart and commitment to make wise choices and place your interest as a representative for them on top of their priority list. You are about to choose the vehicle to take you down the road to financial freedom, so choose wisely!

THINK IT OVER...

Use this list to take an inventory of your personal product category preferences—you will be glad you took this step first! Below is a partial list of product/service categories that use the network marketing business model. Circle the ones that you currently use and love or that you would be interested in learning more about, then spend some time researching them online.

Accessories/Handbags	Fragrances	Photography/Photo Processing
Air Filtration Systems	Garden Accessories	Plants/Foliage
Animal/Pet Care	Giftware	Real Estate Services
Aromatherapy	Greeting Cards/Gifts	Religious Books/Gifts
Art/Framing	Group Buying Service	Rubber Stamps
Audio/CDs/Cassettes	Hair Care	Scrapbooking/
Auto Care	Health/Fitness/Wellness	Photo Albums
Baby/Childcare	Holiday Decorations	Security Systems
Baskets	Home Appliances	Skincare
Benefits Packages	Home Décor	Software/Computers
Books	Home Technology	Spa Products
Brokerage Services	Homecare	Specialty Beverages
Candles	Homeopathies	Sporting Goods
Clothing/Shoes	House & Kitchenware	Tableware
Coffee/Tea	Insurance	Telecommunications Services
Specialty Beverages	Internet Services	Tools
Cookware	Jewelry	Toys/Games
Cosmetics	Legal Services	Travel
Crafts/Craft Supplies	Lingerie/Sleepwear	Utilities
Crystal/China	Nutritional Supplements	Vacuum Cleaners
Cutlery	Oral Hygiene	Videos
Encyclopedias	Paper Products	Water Treatment Systems
Financial Services	Party Supplies	Weight Management
Food/Gourmet Items	Personal Care	Wine/Wine Accessories

CHAPTER 3

Set Your Internal GPS

We have focused up to this point on the importance of belief in:

1) The network marketing business model
2) Your product and your company

There is, however, one more area of belief that is even more important: Belief in YOU!

The most important key to success in your network marketing business is inside yourself!

The secret to success in Network Marketing has been called many things, including "mindset" and the "inner game." However you name it, it is composed of two things, both hugely important.

HAVE A BIG DREAM—YOUR "WHY"

Now is the time to retrieve your dreams from the back of the closet, dust them off, and make them shine again. What is your goal or "Big Dream" in your mind of what you want your life to look like at the end of your network marketing career? Your Dream can be whatever you choose, but it should be BIG and definitely bigger than you, involving others who become part of your vision and help you carry it out.

Your Big Dream could involve making the world a better place because of your products/services or funding a non-profit with the proceeds. For example, your dream might involve others in the following ways:
- Helping people with their health issues
- Helping people raise their self-esteem
- Setting up a nonprofit foundation
- Helping children around the world
- Funding an animal rescue organization

Your Big Dream should include your family, and it should visualize helping them have a better life by sharing in your financial success. Examples could include:
- Retiring your hard-working spouse from his/her job
- Financing your children's college education
- Setting up a trust fund for your grandchildren

Another word for your Big Dream is your *"WHY."* Your *why* is your Big Reason for making a commitment to start a new business, learn new skills, put in consistent hours for a few years, and overcome the inevitable bumps in the road and even some detours on the highway to financial freedom. Your *why* has to be big enough and strong enough to handle any temporary setback that is put in your path—every obstacle and all forms of negativity, internal and external, that threaten to derail your Dream—make it Big!

Judy's Big Dream: Inspire millions of baby boomers to achieve financial freedom and live their retirement dreams through the principles and action steps outlined in this book. Visit every state in the USA in my new RV and support my team members along the way. As my company expands internationally, get paid to spread our model of financial freedom to women worldwide.

Kristi's Big Dream: Empower and inspire women around the planet financially, emotionally, and spiritually so they can teach their children to do the same. Empower and inspire people in the corporate world so they can reclaim their lives and create massive wealth for their family and future generations.

Karen's Big Dream: Empower women, especially moms, to embrace their desires to be present in their homes, while still pursuing their passions and utilizing their gifts to help others. Be completely financially free and enjoy the freedom to put my family first. To support the ministries that are near and dear to my heart—caring for orphans and providing clean water for children around the world.

Here's a tip to help you:

Before you get started, make a Vision Board with visual reminders of your *why*. You can get poster board or foam board from any craft or office supply store. Cut out pictures from magazines representing your Big Dream and what you want for yourself and your family and paste them on the Vision Board. Involve your children and spouse. Hang it in a prominent place in your home and go back to it often to remind yourself *why* you are doing your business and how you will know when you are done (everything on the Vision Board will have come true!).

The bad news: You will have challenges.

The good news: You don't have to let them block you.

The best news: If your Big Dream is big enough, you will become unstoppable!

BELIEVE IN YOURSELF

The most important thing you must have to create the life of your dreams is belief in yourself. Our reality is created to a large degree by our thoughts, feelings, and belief systems. You may be holding on to negative ideas that could limit your success. If you are stuck in believing that you are a certain way and can't change or grow—"I'm not a good salesperson" or "I couldn't run my own business" or "I just don't have the right personality"—then you are allowing fear-based, negative thoughts to keep you from using your talents and abilities to reach your dreams and find your own greatness.

Your biggest enemy is the committee of negative voices inside you. They are just a bunch of fear-based losers whose only job is to keep you stuck in your current comfort zone of the familiar, and keep you from risking failure by trying something new. Their voices might sound like this:

- "But you have no sales experience."
- "But you're too _____ (old, young, shy, dumb, etc.) to be a success."
- "What if you fail?"
- "What if it doesn't work?"

Here's a reality check: You are limited only by your fear of the new and unknown. What if it DOES work, and you could create financial freedom for yourself and your family? What if you missed out on your shot at your dreams because you were too afraid to try? THAT would be the only real way to fail!

You don't need experience to be successful. You will receive all the training you need from your company and the person or group that introduced you to the business. When we started out, we had no sales training and no experience. What you do need are:

- A product/service you love
- A desire to share it
- A passion to help others
- Basic company training and education from your team leaders on how to succeed
- Willingness to grow and step out of the traditional ways of thinking and being that may have limited you in the past.

Every one of us has the capability of being successful, helping many others along the way, and making a tremendous contribution to the world. Don't allow the "committee" to steal your dream! Take the first steps, have faith in yourself and all you are capable of, and your greatness will begin to unfold as the path to your dreams appears beneath your feet—one step at a time. You will have many people to help and guide you along the way, and you will grow in ways you can't even imagine.

Network marketing is a wonderful and rewarding venture that can change your life and the lives of your family forever.

KEY POINT

BELIEVE that you can do it and be successful—because YOU CAN!

DETOUR—WOMEN ONLY

Belief in yourself is so important to success in network marketing and in life. Because many women struggle with issues related to self esteem and self-worth, we will focus briefly on issues that are especially likely to affect women. Some are cultural, a result of society's norms and gender roles, even in these modern times. Most are a result of how we are raised and the messages we still receive about "how to be" in the world.

If you do not relate to any of the examples, feel free to skip this section. If you do relate to one or more of the stories regarding issues that can sabotage you, we encourage you to not let the issue block your progress, either personally or in your business. Through your own conscious effort and support from others, you can overcome any limiting beliefs from your past. Your network marketing business can be your vehicle to personal transformation of anything that is keeping you from fully participating in life's abundance.

You deserve it—don't let anything hold you back!

JUDY'S STORY

In my own experience, as well as my 25 years of being a women's counselor, I have seen so many women (especially of my Baby Boomer generation—but not limited to that age range) who grew up feeling their needs always came last on "the list." We were told it was a good thing to go to college and prepare for a career, yet in the same breath the ultimate goal was to find a "nice boy" and get married. If that marriage were to take place, it superseded any plans for a career—the husband's needs came first.

Of course, when women became mothers, the needs of the children and the family came first, and this would go on for 20 years or more until the last child was grown and out of the home. I am not suggesting that this is wrong—only that as women (particularly Baby Boomer women) we have never been taught to value our own needs. I worked with hundreds of women to correct this limiting belief in my career.

Today I see many women still struggling with their own value and the importance of their needs in running their home-based business. They feel guilty leaving their family for evening trainings or taking time away to make follow-up calls or meeting someone to introduce to their product or service. I can assure you, men do not struggle with this issue and have no problem asserting their needs!

If you can relate to this situation, it is important to have other women in your life who believe in your right to have your own needs, and who will gently confront you when you get off track and fall back into limited ways of thinking about your worth and value. This could be your best friend, a women's support group, the person who introduced you to your network marketing company (your "sponsor"), a coach, or even a counselor. The important thing is to have other women in your life who believe in your dream and your ability to achieve it—and will gently (or not!) encourage you to go for it, helping to override "the committee."

BARBARA'S STORY

Like many women, Barbara was raised to be polite, and saying "no" was considered rude. Being assertive and setting boundaries with others was not OK. Many women are raised with the importance of being liked, of having others outside themselves approve of them to feel OK about themselves. For some women, self-worth comes from without instead of from within.

These limiting beliefs affected Barbara in her network marketing career, despite her success. She found it difficult to say "no." She is a hard worker and a leader, but struggles with setting boundaries. For example, when she hosts team events and trainings in her home, people stay longer than expected and Barbara finds it difficult to tell them it's time to leave. She does a lot of team support and training on the phone, but struggles with telling people when they are getting off the subject and staying on the phone too long, keeping her from more productive activities. Her husband doesn't like her to be away from him at night to build her business, and this causes her internal stress. She finds it hard to establish boundaries around her time, as it might disappoint others. In spite of these limitations, Barbara has become a success in her company—and she is working to overcome her limiting beliefs about taking control of her time. When she does, her success will be that much greater.

KORI'S STORY

Kori and her husband are rising stars in their company, shooting into the Top 25 Distributor list in a relatively short period of time. Yet, like many women who are part of a husband-wife team working their network marketing business together, Kori would often hang back from being in the limelight, deferring to her husband and seeing herself in his shadow. Then she took a company-sponsored trip without him for the first time. Here is what she discovered in her own words:

"Even though my husband and I are business partners, I discovered that I was not treating him as an equal partner, but as the stronger, wiser, more informative partner. I not only looked to him for guidance, but also would direct our team members and customers to him for the more challenging questions within our business. What I found on my trip without him was that when I was asked the same questions that I would usually direct to my husband, the answers flowed from me like water!"

From that experience, Kori found her own voice and realized she had the same level of knowledge and skill as her husband. She made the commitment to herself to value herself equally to her husband in expertise and step into her own power and greatness. Now Kori has become an example to the other women in her business. What an incredible lesson!

JODI'S STORY

Jodi is an example of a woman who grew up with self-doubt and limiting beliefs about herself. Her internal "committee" told her for years, "You aren't the woman you SHOULD be."

Jodi's insecurities about herself manifested outwardly in a quest for perfection. She had a need to always have her home look perfect and her children always be perfectly behaved. She was trying to control everything on the outside to make up for feelings of "not good enough" on the inside. Can you imagine how hard it would be to run a successful home-based business with these thoughts?

Finally, after much internal struggle, Jodi spent one entire day mentally and emotionally LETTING GO of her old ideas of who she should be, with anger and tears released along with her old thinking patterns. At the end of this purposeful release, Jodi was able to replace those old limiting beliefs with ones that told her "You are OK just the way you are—just be yourself." Jodi's world has been a much more harmonious place ever since.

Would it surprise you to know that this woman is the wife of a CEO of a network marketing company? This is proof that self-doubt and insecurity can affect any woman—from the CEO's wife to the brand new distributor. Learning to let go and replace the limiting beliefs of our internal "committee" is the universal solution, as Jodi's story illustrates.

If you relate to any of these issues of people-pleasing, perfectionism, inability to say, "no," or set boundaries, or always putting your needs on hold for others, it is so important to reach out for help. Don't allow your dreams to be sabotaged by your old limiting beliefs!

We challenge you to use your network marketing business as your vehicle—not just for financial freedom, but also for the growth and personal empowerment that will make it all possible.

You deserve it!

THINK IT OVER...

What are some of your Big Dreams?

How can your dreams help your family?

How can your dreams make the world a better place?

What are some of the limiting beliefs that may be holding you back?

Who can help you identify and let go of your limiting beliefs?

List some positive affirmations here to help you overcome those beliefs. (We'll give you a few to get started.)

I am financially free!

I am a talented, creative woman who is attracting positive people to join me in my business!

I am achieving my dreams!

I am _____

I am _____

I am _____

I am _____

CHAPTER 4

Creating a Road Map

GOALS ARE A PATHWAY TO YOUR DREAMS!

For many successful entrepreneurs, "what you believe, you can achieve" is the mantra they credit for their success. The image you have in your mind of who you are and what your future looks like is drawing you forward. Your dream, your vision of your future, is your *why*. That *why* keeps you focused and on course.

As important as having a dream is, it's also vital to chart your course by setting goals for yourself, because goals guide your actions. Affirmation without action is useless. If you think of your dream as your final destination, your goals are the stops you'll make along the way. Goals are like a road map of your future.

Sometimes it's not easy to keep your eyes on your goals, but if you do, you will get where you want to go. Whether you are driving, walking a balance beam, or working toward your *why*, you have to stay focused on where you are going.

Let's say that you are planning a road trip from San Diego to New York. Would you simply dream of New York—visualize yourself there and magically open your eyes to find yourself on Fifth Avenue? No! While you need to know where you're going, you also have to chart a course to get there. Do you want to take the scenic route? The quickest route? Go by foot, car, train, or air? Who are you going to bring with you? What are you going to bring with you? How long do you want the trip to take? Obviously, answering these questions ahead of time is going to make your trip a much more enjoy-able experience, as well as ensure that you will actually make it to your destination. Your goals should reflect both your stops along the way (promotions, income goals, etc), and the actions you need to take to get there.

Interestingly, you can also control the speed of your vehicle simply by keeping your eyes on the vehicle ahead of you. You automatically pace yourself. Find someone to look up to—a role model. Follow where they are going, do what they are doing, and you will get to where they are! How fast are they going? What are they achieving?

MAKING GOOD PROMISES

There is a formula to follow that will help you make SMART goals or promises—the acronym SMART.

S = Specific

First, you have to be specific about what you want to accomplish. Saying, "I want to have lots of money" isn't specific enough, just as saying, "I'm going across the country," isn't specific enough. Do you want to go to New York state or New York City? What hotel are you stay-ing at? A better goal would be, "I'm going to the Man-hattan Club on Sixth Street in New York City so I can visit x, y, and z!" (Hint—the x, y, and z would be your Dream!)

For your business, you'll want to think about your dream and then choose your goals accordingly. Think about the milestones you need to achieve before you get to your dream life. What promotions do you need to achieve? How about a specific dollar amount you want to be earning each month? A certain number of team members or customers? Those would be your stops along the way. Your food and gasoline stops would be your actions—how many phone calls do you need to make? How many new people do you need to meet? Set specific benchmarks for yourself and specify EXACTLY what your goals are.

As women, we tend to be too nice about saying what we want. We might agree to go to a restaurant we don't like to keep harmony in our relationships or buy a dress because someone else thinks it looks great. If you can't articulate what you want in your business, you won't be able to get there. Choose your own goals and state them clearly visually and in writing!

M = Measurable

If we look again at our hypothetical trip to New York, we can easily measure our journey in several ways. We can calculate how many miles the trip is, how long it will take to travel, and how much money it will cost. At any point along the way, we can easily measure our progress. We can keep track of our mileage, our time, and our expenses and see how far we've come and how we are progressing toward our destination.

In terms of your business, you can measure how many team members and customers you need to get to your first promotion. You can then take a step back at any time and measure your progress. If you need to earn x amount of dollars each month, you can easily track how close you are to achieving your goal.

Are you afraid to weigh yourself because you might not like what you see? Sometimes we have to face up to our failures in order to overcome them—creating measurable goals helps us to do that. And, you never know, maybe you've gone farther than you thought!

A = Attainable

The third characteristic of a good goal is that it's attainable. A road trip to New York from San Diego is certainly attainable, as is your success in your network marketing career. However, neither goal is attainable **overnight**. The farther away your dream is from your current location, the more intermediate stops you want to plan, because setting unattainable goals only sets you up for disappointment.

In your company, your dream might be to get to the highest level in the company. However, that's not something you can achieve in one day. Some of your progress might depend on your own efforts, while other parts may depend on teaching and training your team. A more attainable goal would be achieving your first promotion. Maybe you want to give yourself six months to get there. That is a very specific, measurable, AND attainable goal. Find out what it takes to get to the first promotion in your company and set that as your goal.

Setting unattainable goals makes us feel like we've failed, and many people give up instead of reevaluating their goals. If you find that you've overreached, that's OK—just take a step back and readjust. Remember that your highest dreams are possible, and to get there you need to take the first step.

R = Realistic

Just as you need to choose goals that are attainable, you also want to choose goals that are realistic. Maybe you only have one hour a day to travel to New York. Is it realistic to say you will get there in one day? Of course not. You know yourself and what you can do. While you should always try to stretch yourself, you also want to be realistic about what you can accomplish within a certain timeframe.

If you can only talk to one person a week, it may not be realistic to get to your first promotion in six months. Maybe it will take you a year. That's OK. It's better to set a realistic goal than one that looks good. In fact, most people in network marketing companies begin to see a full-time income after three to five years. Especially if you are new to our business model and already have a full-time job or you are a stay at home mom with other responsibilities, it may take longer to get there. Just stick with it and remember that realistically, it will take you a few years to get to where you want to go. Remember, too, that most people overestimate what they can do in the short term, but underestimate what they can do in the long term. Keep your dreams big, and your goals realistic.

That is not to say that you should hold yourself back. It's better to set your goals just a little out of reach, because you will move farther along your path if you need to push yourself a little bit. In a seminar, Michael Bernhoff explained it this way: "You will rarely go past the goal you've set for yourself." In fact, we usually just get to the line. If you want to run one mile, do you ever think that you'll just go for a little more once you get there, or do you find yourself slowing down when the finish line is in sight? Set realistic goals that make you stretch just a little bit.

T = Timeline

Goals must have a timeline! Take our trip to New York, for example. Let's say that we have a complete plan of action for getting there. We've decided on the route we want to take. We know how much it's going to cost. We know where we want to stay. But we never set a date for completing our trip. Will we ever get there? Maybe. But our trip will be much more successful if we set our arrival date in advance. It's the same with your business. The pace you set for yourself is determined by your timeline. So the final step is to look at your goals and set a timeline.

I HAVE MY GOALS, WHAT NOW?

Having your goals is one thing. Now you have to know how to use these goals effectively. Otherwise, they will go in the pile with all those New Year's resolutions that are made and forgotten within a few weeks. How can you keep your goals an ongoing part of your life?

Internalize them

Much like you do with your dreams, you need to internalize your goals—they should become a part of you, and you need to train your subconscious mind to move toward those goals by stating them over and over again in present tense as if they are happening right NOW. For example, "I am in New York City at the Manhattan Club on December 14, 2010."

Is this a magic formula? Maybe! Constantly feeding your mind with positive affirmations reflecting the goals you've made will have an exponential impact on your business and your quality of life. Jordan Rubin, author of *The Maker's Diet,* says, "In most cases, the things you

do and say begin with the things you think and believe."
So imagine if, instead of telling yourself over and over,
I'm broke! I'm fat! I'm a loser! you begin telling yourself, *I am earning $500 extra each month! I am healthy
and fit!* and *I am a winner!* Can you feel the difference
in your attitude just reading the statements? Imagine
what could change if you made those positive statements a part of your everyday life!

Say them out loud

We believe that the power of speaking words out
loud is greatly underappreciated. If you say your goals/
affirmations out loud every day, you're giving the words
power to act in your life. You need to feed yourself your
affirmations out loud daily as "I am" statements, and
you'll find that you not only have a better outlook on life,
but that you're making progress toward your goals and
ultimately your dream.

Masuru Emoto is a Japanese scientist whose belief
that water is living prompted him to experiment with
the effect of words on water. He would take samples of
water and speak words of love to one sample and words
of hate to the other. Then he froze the samples. Under a
microscope, the frozen water he spoke lovingly to made
beautiful, symmetrical crystals. On the other hand, the
water he spoke hatefully to formed twisted, ugly shapes.

As a woman, it's particularly important to beware of
the words you accept into your life. Our words are not
just the key to communication. They are the source of
power—for good or for evil. We've all been the recipients
of words that lift us up and words that bring us down.
Speak only words to yourself that will lift you up—and
do the same for the people in your life.

Write them down

An old story says that in 1979, a group of business students at Harvard were interviewed about their business goals. The students were grouped into three categories: Those who wrote down their goals, those who made verbal goals, and those with no goals. Eighty-four percent of the students had no goals at all. Ten years later, the three percent who had written down their goals were earning ten times the other 97 percent combined. By writing down your goals, you are bringing your dreams to life.

Everyone has heard of Jim Carrey, but you may not know about the goal he made for himself. As a struggling actor in 1987, he wrote himself a check for $10 million and dated the check for Thanksgiving of 1995, with a notation that the check was for acting services rendered. Guess what? By the time the date on the check rolled around in 1995, Carrey's movies had made millions, and his price per picture was up to $20 million. That's the power of a SMART goal written down!

Once you've written your goals, you need to place them somewhere that you can review them daily. We also suggest putting pictures with your goals whenever possible—remember your vision board? This gives your mind both visual and verbal reminders of where you want to go.

Find an accountability partner

So many of us set great goals for ourselves, but keep them a secret. Why? Just in case...just in case we fail! We might say that we'll surprise others with the results of our secret diet, but the more likely outcome is that no one will ever know we're on a diet, so we have no reason to succeed—or even try!

It is vital to find someone who you can share your goals with, and who will help keep you accountable for taking the actions necessary to achieve those goals. Whether this person is a friend, a family member, or someone in your company, it is so important that you find someone to work with. Connect with them regularly to share your struggles and your successes. Together, you will help each other achieve your dreams. As women, one of our strongest talents is the ability to network and build and foster relationships. Take advantage of your natural desire to work with someone, and you and your partner will help each other reach new heights.

FINAL THOUGHTS

Goals are meant to be achieved. But achieving a goal is not the end. Review your goals at least every quarter so that you can adjust them according to your circumstances. If you've accomplished something, great! Set your sights on the next stop on your journey.

What if you don't achieve a goal in the timeline you set for yourself? So what? Having that deadline probably pushed you to achieve more and work harder than if you hadn't set that goal. Not meeting a goal is not a failure; it's simply not meeting a goal. If you fall down, you've got to get up and go at it again. Like a child learning to ride a bike, we have two choices: We can choose to be cynical and just give up, or we can choose to be creative and move forward.

Goals are just destinations along the road to your dream. Sometimes we get there ahead of schedule, and sometimes we run a little behind. No big deal. Sometimes there's even a detour. No problem! Just keep your eyes on your big dream, and keep checking in on your progress. If you run into a challenge, chart a new course.

There is an old saying that the journey of 1,000 miles begins with a single step. Each day we choose with our words what journey we will begin. We choose the paths our lives will take. Choose your life's direction with care. Stop saying, "I hope to someday" and make a decision today to take action and move forward to create your Dream Life.

THINK IT OVER...

List some goals you have already achieved.

What are some ways you can implement the concepts in this chapter?

If you are in a business already, list some SMART goals.

Who is a potential accountability partner for you?

Chapter 5

Wear Your Seatbelt—Family Support

For women, especially, a support network is vital. We already have so much on our plates—work, family, household. With all of that going on, building a new business, no matter how important it is to you and your future, can easily fall to the wayside if you don't have the support of the people closest to you. For many of us, that support will come from our families; for others, your biggest support will be from your friends or from someone you've only just met in your new company.

IMPORTANCE OF FAMILY SUPPORT

As women, one of the most important reasons we (Judy, Kristi, and Karen) decided to build a business with network marketing is our families. We wanted more time to be with them. To all of us, it is important to be able to set our own schedules so that we can enjoy time with our families, instead of being constantly stressed out and pushing them aside.

If you're like us, your dream or your *why* also has a lot to do with your family. Maybe, like Karen, you want to be a stay-at-home mom who is truly home. Maybe you want time to spend with your grandkids or your spouse. Don't lose sight of the most important people in your life as you pursue your new business.

Without the support of the people closest to you, you may begin to lose your excitement about your dreams. If they are on board with you, then you keep each other excited. Your family can encourage you and provide you with a natural accountability source as you look forward to living your dreams together. Besides, it's so much more fun to do things with someone you love than to do them on your own!

INVOLVING YOUR SPOUSE

One of the best ways to involve your spouse is to dream big together. Take some time with your spouse and get away—even if it's just a walk around your neighborhood or a dinner out. Talk about what you want from life. What are your dreams? Sometimes dreams that seem impossible when they are in your head suddenly become very real when you share them with someone who is close to you. Make sure that you give your spouse time to share his dreams, too. If he can see how your new business can empower him, too, he is more likely to be supportive, if not actively helping you in your business.

We recently heard a story about a woman who is building a massive network marketing team in India. She advises women there not to tell their spouses about their business until they get their first check because in general, women are not supposed to be in business in that country. That way, they can overcome many of the objections and show that they have already been successful. We do NOT advise you to keep secrets from your family, but do be patient with any doubters. As you start to reap the benefits of your efforts, they may become more positive.

When you begin your business, and every quarter as you reevaluate your progress, take time to make goals together. What do you want to accomplish and when? If you work together to formulate goals, then you are more likely to achieve them. Not only are you making a verbal agreement about what you will do, but you have constant accountability through your spouse. Again, make sure that your goals take into account both of your dreams.

Building a business does take work, and it does take time. As you make your goals, think about when you want to meet those deadlines and how much time you will need. Work together to formulate a family schedule. You'd be surprised how much time you have during the day when you sit and plan out an hourly schedule. It really is worth it! That way, you know who is doing what, and when. Even if your spouse is not actively involved in your business, at least he knows when you are planning to work and will be better able to accommodate you. If you don't make these decisions together, you may find that you have conflicts or confusion that could easily have been avoided simply by working together.

Once you've agreed upon a schedule, you need to write it down or, even better, post it somewhere for everyone in the house to see. If you have small children at home, you can put up a brightly colored poster, Super Nanny style. Having a written schedule brings stability and predictability to your home, which is especially important for young children.

INVOLVING YOUR CHILDREN

Children do well when they have a predictable schedule and know what is going on in their lives. A family schedule is great for keeping your family on track, but it also helps the kids to know where they are in their day. They know when they get time with mommy and daddy, what their chores are, etc. It gives them power over their day and their lives.

Allowing your kids to dream big with you also empowers them. Make your dreams a favorite family topic of conversation. Your kids are another reason to make a dream board. You can get a piece of poster board for less than a dollar and print off pictures of your dreams from your computer. Better yet, give your children scissors and a stack of magazines and help them dream big! (In fact, you might learn a thing or two from their unlimited imaginations.) Let your kids glue or tape the pictures to the poster board, and then display it.

Helping kids set goals teaches them the importance of sticking with it, managing their money, saving, and the list goes on and on. Our children learn from us, and building a business from home provides us with so many teachable moments. We can raise our children to be natural entrepreneurs. Karen's six-year-old daughter decided she wanted an American Girl baby doll. She made a goal chart and kept track of her progress, finally earning close to $100 needed to buy her doll. At eight, she decided to do it again, and is getting ready to buy her second American Girl doll.

Children can also be involved in the day to day reality of business building. They can put labels on brochures and other promotional materials. They can stamp and put address labels on envelopes and help keep you organized. Bring your kids with you to networking events and personal development seminars, as Kristi and Karen often do. They will learn the importance of hard work, good listening skills, and valuable entrepreneurial skills like goal setting and networking.

While there are many opportunities to involve your children in your business, at times you will be unable to do so. If you can't afford a babysitter, don't be afraid to ask for help from family members or team members. You can even offer to trade babysitting with a team member or a family member or pitch in on a sitter for big team events.

Remember, the goal is to build your business without neglecting your kids. Always make an effort to spend quality time with your children. You might schedule family time every evening and be sure to eat all of your meals together. Sit outside with your children as you check email in the afternoon, and take a break to have a Popsicle or a snack. Even sitting at a table with them while they do their homework and you work on your business creates a feeling of companionship. Sharing little special moments with your kids can make a big difference in their attitudes toward you and in their own self-esteem.

Outside the home, you can also include your children by taking them with you to networking events or business trips. If you do take your kids with you on business trips, try to stay a day or two longer to spend time as a family, to incorporate some really fun family memories into every trip.

Despite all the fun ways you can incorporate your children into your business life, it's important to set aside family days when no work is allowed. That doesn't necessarily mean that you play all day, but spend time together working in the garden or going to garage sales or doing whatever it is that your family enjoys. You might also give your children a special day when the kids choose what they want to do. Whether they like going to get ice cream or having a movie night, setting aside family time makes everyone happy.

With the uncertainty of the economy around us, we as parents also have even more of an obligation to prepare our children to have an entrepreneurial spirit to create their own economy.

KRISTI'S STORY—PART 1

I became a single mom when my daughter Jade was three years old. My immediate family lives out of state, so there were times when it was necessary to bring Jade to meetings. Here are some of the things I did to train Jade about the importance of sitting quietly through networking meetings:

1. Pack a "fun bag" with age-appropriate quiet toys (puzzles, coloring books, stickers, stuffed animals).

2. Bring snacks, a drink in a spill-proof cup, baby wipes.

3. Set your child up for success by letting her know what to expect ("The room will look like this, there will be people on our team there, if you want to come back with me to another meeting, you will need to use your manners.")

4. Teach your child about the importance of business cards ("This is how people will be able to call us to learn more about our business.") Business cards are never used to draw on—they mean money to our family.

5. Use positive reinforcement ("I really like the way you are sitting quietly—you are such a big girl.")

6. Make sure to have your child use the bathroom before you leave for the meeting, and make sure to sit closest to the bathroom so you don't interrupt the meeting in case she has to go again.

7. Teach your child to look someone in the eye, shake hands, and say, "Nice to meet you."

8. Do something fun, such as allowing your child to choose a reward for sitting quietly and using manners.

9. Teach the importance of being prepared and on time. There was a weekly networking meeting I attended that began at 7 a.m., before Jade's school started. I taught her how we prepared by putting our things by the door the night before (purse, car keys, business cards, product samples, her fun bag, and backpack for school). We set out clothes the night before, and I reinforced the importance of getting enough sleep. I taught her the reason we did that is that we didn't want to be like the white rabbit in Alice in Wonderland that ran around saying "I'm late, I'm late, for a very important date." To this day, at age eight, she can wake up, be dressed and ready to go in 15 minutes, with a great attitude.

I faced fewer objections about meetings from my daughter the minute I started calling her "my business partner" and talking to her about "our team." We keep track of our team count on a white board in our office, and Jade gets to change the number each time someone joins our team.

SHOW APPRECIATION

One of the most vital things we can do as women is show appreciation for our families and for the people who are helping us achieve our goals. Send thank you notes to your babysitters and the family members who are supporting you. Send a card to your kids telling them how great they are. Most importantly, make sure your spouse knows how much his support means to you.

When you show your appreciation in tangible ways, people know you care about them and that you aren't just using them to achieve your own ends, and are more willing to continue supporting you.

WHAT IF YOU DON'T HAVE FAMILY?

What if you don't have family? What if your spouse isn't interested in your business? Or if you are a single mom? Find someone in your life who will support you. Whether this someone is a friend or a family member or someone on your team, it's vital to have an accountability partner. In fact, if you don't have a friend or family member who will support you in your goals, a team member is a perfect choice. Share your dreams with them. Write down your goals and give them a copy so they can keep you accountable. You can work together to build a team. Go to networking events together, trade babysitting, and spend time together dreaming and making goals. Remember, your support system is vital to your success.

TAKE TIME TO BE YOU

Throughout this book we have been using the metaphor of driving your car to your destination of financial freedom. There are many women out there—it might even be you—who are courageously taking steps toward improving themselves (going back to school, learning a skill, working outside the home, or starting a home-based business). You may experience the thrill of starting your own business; you have customers buying your product or service, and you have team members who are starting to work the business with you. Your paychecks start rolling in.

As you gain confidence, your energy will start to be different, and—guess what? This starts to change the "script" in your personal relationships. Most of your family members and friends will be drawn to your increased vitality and self-confidence—they will want what you have. But, if you are in an abusive relationship, your spouse or significant other will recognize that your business is not a hobby, and the fear of losing control over you may start the sabotage of your business.

It's important to recognize who you really are. There is a saying "You can't move forward until you know where you've been." For you to step into your greatness, you need to be true to yourself. Find a quiet place and look inside yourself—when was the last time you were truly happy? We as women tend to take care of everyone else first and many times never get around to taking care of ourselves. If you don't take time to refill your cup, and you keep pouring yourself out to those you love and care about, you will start to sacrifice your sleep, your personal time, your boundaries, and your health. Much like the oxygen in an airplane, if you don't take care of yourself first, you won't be able to help anyone else.

This applies especially to building a successful network marketing business—you cannot help everyone grow their business and neglect continuing to have your own personal enrollments. Heal from the inside out and all aspects of your life will start to get in harmony.

DETOUR: WHAT IF YOUR SPOUSE OR SIGNIFICANT OTHER IS ABUSIVE? KRISTI'S STORY—PART 2

I was married for almost 17 years. There were signs while we were dating that he had anger issues—the blow-ups, followed by apologies, and being treated sweetly...until the next time. I chose to ignore the "red flags" because we had more good times than bad. And after all, he loved me, and didn't that outweigh the negative stuff? I was successful in my career, getting promotion after promotion and overseeing people and projects, and yet when it came to my personal life, it was a mess.

Women will compartmentalize their personal and business lives as if they are two different people. One day, my best friend sat me down and said, "I want you to read these questions and answer them—I am going to stay right here while you do." It was a series of questions that identified being in an abusive relationship. I looked at her and said, "I'm not in an abusive relationship—he has never hit me." But as I read through the questions, and many more were "yes" than "no," I was sobbing by the time I got to the end. I didn't realize that abuse isn't just physical, that it can be emotional, financial, spiritual, mental. That's not something we are taught in school, and certainly not something that is taught at home. It took me several more years to gain the courage and confidence to finally leave.

As our marriage was coming to an end, so was my corporate career of 20 years in marketing and retail—my company was moving out of state (what would have been my fourth move), and my gut feeling was that the move was just a strategy to buy time with the stockholders. I shared with my husband that I wanted to start my own business, utilizing the 20 years of experience I had learned to become a marketing consultant, to help companies analyze what they are doing, make suggestions, and get results. Here was his response: "What is your Plan B if you fail?" It was then I knew I had to leave this marriage or I would never be able to spread my wings and truly soar.

At first, I resisted getting professional counseling for many reasons; I felt I could handle it on my own, it was just one more "failure" that I needed to seek help about, I would have to be vulnerable in front of a stranger. I went through three counselors before I found one who was a good fit. He was instrumental in helping me get through this very difficult, emotional time in my life.

Just about the same time, a life coach in my BNI group, Lauren Kelly, was teaching a Women's Emotional Wellness class. Lauren taught us about safe and unsafe boundaries, relationships, choices, the different phases of shame, and much more. One of the most revealing things I learned was that I was unsafe within myself, and, therefore, attracting unsafe relationships— ouch! That was not something I was expecting to learn. However, the old saying, "When the student is ready, the teacher appears," was so true in my case. We started out with a class of 12, and, by the time we graduated, we were left with six. Again, this was not an easy class to take—you have to be willing to do the work within, if you want to benefit on the outside. If you are in a similar place, I encourage you to seek help from a qualified counselor, and make a commitment to stick with it so you can be free.

THINK IT OVER...

How might your family react to your decision to start a business?

How can you involve your spouse in your new business?

In what ways could your children be part of your business?

What entrepreneurial skills could you teach your children?

Who in your life can you rely on for support? List your potential support network here.

List five ways you will take care of yourself while you are building your business.

Chapter 6

Read the Manual

It's important to learn all you can about network marketing if you truly want to succeed: You must become a lifelong student. Successful network marketers become experts in their fields. When you listen to a conference call or hear a successful network marketer speak, many times they drop the same names, quote the same quotes, and read the same books as other successful entrepreneurs. Whether the subject is sales or personal development, when successful people get together, they're talking about the new idea they heard or the new concept they learned. They not only know the information, but it's what they think about and talk about. It permeates them and becomes a part of who they are.

These successful entrepreneurs have discovered a secret: To share your product or service effectively, you have to believe in it yourself. If you aren't totally sold on network marketing, on your company, on your product, even on yourself, no one else will be, either. If you want to be successful, you have to have confidence in these four areas. That confidence comes through knowledge. This isn't knowledge the successful entrepreneurs were born with—and it's not exclusive to them. You have the ability to gain the same knowledge and perspective by educating yourself. If you spend the time to learn more and become a better you, then you can also become an expert and have massive success in your business. There is an old saying, "If you want more—become more than you are!"

When people choose to buy your product or join in your business, they are not only buying the company and the product—they are buying YOU! Network marketing is a "people business." It involves connecting with people, finding and meeting their needs, building relationships, and building teams. As you become a student of sales and relationships, you make yourself a valuable team member and then a leader. Not only will this help you help your team, but it will help you grow your business. Become a student of personal growth. The better you become, the faster your business will grow.

WHERE DO I BEGIN

"OK," you say, "I get it. I need to learn all of this stuff. But how? I'm new to this business. I don't even know where to begin!" The first place to look is within your company. Every company wants its distributors to be successful, and they usually have a list of resources to help you do just that. Find out what books and magazines your company recommends. Watch all the training videos available on your website and read through your training materials thoroughly. Ask questions about anything you don't understand or want to learn more about.

CORPORATE CALLS

Find out when the corporate calls are and listen in. You'll find new and relevant information on your company and your products. Not only that, but many companies highlight their top producers in the calls; perhaps you'll get to learn some of their best strategies for building a business. This is an area many people neglect. You can be one of the first people in your organization with the latest developments in your company. Get on those calls!

TEAM LEADER CALLS

In addition to corporate calls, you will be part of a team. Each team has a leader who typically has been in the business for a few years and achieved a level of success. Very often, he/she will host weekly conference calls for their entire team. These calls can be a treasure—a wealth of training tips and "how to's" for building your new business. Get on these calls whenever possible, and listen to the recordings later if you miss them. Take notes—this is your education, your "classroom," and you will be learning from people who didn't just read about network marketing—they are out there proving it works.

COMPANY CONVENTION

Most companies also hold annual conventions. Traveling to the convention and booking a hotel room may seem expensive, but it's worth it. Even better, bring your team with you. Top leaders say that each person who attends a convention adds 100 new people to their team over time. Why is that? Leverage. For every person you bring who experiences the training and invaluable networking at your convention, many hours of your valuable time training and motivating them yourself will be saved. You also have the opportunity to meet company representatives and top achievers in person. You hear motivational speakers, and you learn how the company is doing. In addition, you get to learn about new products and the vision for the company. Most importantly, you meet others who are excited about what they're doing and who can share ideas with you. You learn and are motivated on many levels, and you bring that motivation back with you—and so does your team!

REGIONAL & LOCAL EVENTS

Regional and local events are the next best thing to keep you and your team inspired and to build momentum. There is nothing that compares to the energy in a group setting to keep everyone inspired. The more you can attend and bring your team with you, the more training and motivation to succeed everyone will come away with—and the faster you all will travel on the road to success and freedom.

MENTORS

Another important source of information is your sponsor, the person who introduced you to your company. If your direct sponsor isn't working his/her business actively, keep going up until you find someone who is. Look for someone who inspires you and whom you like. When you choose a mentor, you're learning more than just what they do, you're learning who they are.

Once you've found a mentor within your company, become an active participant in anything they have to offer. Listen to their conference calls. Read their e-mails and blogs. Attend the team meetings they are leading. Go to the seminars they go to. Ask questions, and always, always, introduce yourself. Take a picture with them and send them a card or an email with the picture so they will know who you are. The best network marketers are always looking for someone on their teams to train and mentor. As you get to know each other and develop a relationship, they will want to help you!

Success breeds success. Spend time with successful people in your company, and you will learn to think and act like them. In the process, you'll find yourself becoming successful, too.

BOOKS & MAGAZINES

Outside of your company, there are many great print resources to turn to. Become a subscriber of *Success* Magazine and *Networking Times*. Here are some great books to add to your library:

The Business of the 21st Century, Robert Kiyosaki
Beach Money, Jordan Adler
Your First Year in Network Marketing,
    Mark Yarnell & Rene Reid Yarnell
How to Win Friends and Influence People,
    Dale Carnegie
Mach II With Your Hair On Fire, Richard Brooke
One Minute Networker, Bryan Thayer
Think and Grow Rich, Napoleon Hill
The Slight Edge, Jeff Olson
Spirit Driven Success, Dani Johnson
Big Al Tells All Series, Tom "Big Al" Schreiter
Excuse Me, Your Life Is Waiting, Lynn Grabhorn
How To Sell in the New Economy, Eric Lofholm

Many of these are also available on CD, so you can listen as you drive or go about your day. The books listed here are just a drop in the bucket. The more you read, the better you will become at network marketing!

Additional CDs we recommend include:
The 4-Year Career, Richard Brooke
The Perfect Business, Robert Kiyosaki
The Close & Time Management, Eric Lofholm
Network Marketing Mastermind Series, Art Jonak
The Big Al Collection, Tom "Big Al" Schreiter
Building Your Business, Jim Rohn

COACHING

One of the very best ways to learn more about how to become a successful entrepreneur is to find a professional coach. Even if you have a successful career in the business world, success in network marketing is not guaranteed, as it requires some different skills. Finding a coach who will help you keep on top of your goals and teach you the skills you need in this new arena can make all the difference!

Whether you listen to teleseminars, go in person to workshops, pay for coaching, or subscribe to an email list or phone coaching, finding a coach is important. It's a good idea to ask your sponsor for recommendations. In many companies, the team leaders often have guest speakers on their calls. When you feel a connection to a speaker, invest in whatever they have to offer. Remember, you are investing in yourself!

Many successful coaches offer free calls and seminars, so you can try them out while learning great information. To help you in this area, we'd like to share with you some of our favorites. Keep in mind that each of these coaches has a different personality and a different specialty. It's a good idea to listen in to a free call or take a seminar with them before deciding if you'd like to work with the coach on a long-term basis. Some of our favorite coaches include:

Eric Lofholm
Dani Johnson
Tom "Big Al" Schreiter
Tim Sales
Kim Klaver
Randy Gage
Todd Falcone
Michael Bernhoff

A common quote often heard in our industry is "You need to work harder on yourself than you do on your business." This is true for many reasons, but the most important one is that the better you become as a person, the more amazing people you will attract on your team and the more things of interest you will have to share. Read an inspirational book about overcoming adversity, eat healthy foods and exercise, and take care of your mental, physical, and spiritual well-being on a daily basis. You will be amazed at the results!

Educating yourself, while continuing on with the daily activities of business-building, will help you achieve massive growth personally and in your business. Knowing your industry, your company, your product, and yourself will give you the power to be successful, and personal growth drives the engine of success. Instead of becoming who you want to be, be who you want to become.

A PERSONAL DEVELOPMENT SUCCESS STORY—KAREN'S STORY

I have always been a high achiever, I wanted to make my parents proud, and I wanted to override the negative voices in my head. I got straight A's in school, even graduating with honors from college with both my BA and MA. Even though my friends liked to call me "nerd" and "brain," in junior high school I decided to be a cheerleader, despite the naysayers in my life. I practiced hard and was one of the three seventh-graders who made the team. In high school, I upped my goal and practiced every day the summer before my sophomore year until I was good enough to be chosen as captain of the varsity team for my sophomore, junior, and senior years. I was student body president and held offices in several other clubs. Even at work I excelled, being promoted to shift manager my junior year in high school. I believed that I could do anything I set my mind to—and I always set the bar high.

When I became a mom, I made a choice to be a mother, gladly giving up my career as a college English professor and my dreams to get my PhD, and become an author to be a stay-at-home mom (anyone else ever try to be supermom?). Over the years, though, I found out that while I loved being a mom, my dreams—my passions in life—wouldn't just be shoved under the rug. But somewhere along the way I had let the negative voices override my passion.

When I chose to begin building my network marketing business, I began with trepidation. I didn't have any experience, but I had a lot of determination. I immediately began listening to every team and corporate call I could, and I bought every book recommended by my team leaders. I listened to free seminars and paid for coaching. It was during one coaching session that I found my passions again.

Not only did all of that personal development help me build my business, but it also reconnected me to my dreams. Since then, I have earned two promotions with my company, written two books, and even won some awards! The best part is that because I've rediscovered who I am, I've found a deeper connection to my husband and my kids. I've learned that I can be present in my home while pursuing my passions. I promise you—personal development will change your life and give you a confidence in your dreams that you never knew existed.

THINK ABOUT IT...

How much of a role does personal development play in your life?

What things have you done already that will help you in the area of personal development?

What qualities are important to you in a coach/mentor?

List three ways you can begin to invest in yourself and create a personal development plan.

CHAPTER 7

Fill Your Tank—Finding Contacts

If you want to take a trip, you don't start off with an empty tank. In network marketing, your contacts are the fuel to fill up your tank and keep your business vehicle running. They are your most valuable assets. One of the things our team leader often says is, "The size of your Rolodex determines the size of your paycheck." Network marketing is all about building relationships with people. Here are some tips on building your network.

PEOPLE YOU KNOW (YOUR "WARM" MARKET)

It is widely understood that women are naturally the best networkers—we are more collaborative and usually form relationships easily. Because of this, we have the edge when it comes to creating and building relationships, which is the heart and soul of network marketing.

It is also a fact that most people know an average of at least 200 to 250 people. These are called your "warm market." We recommend you begin with your warm market contacts, as they already know you and have rapport with you.

In fact, when you start your new business, one of the first things to do is let your friends, family, and colleagues know about your product. Here is the good part—you already have a comfort level in talking with them, and if you sincerely let them know that you would like to practice with them in talking about your product/

service, they are more likely to give you grace while you get comfortable. This will help you gain the confidence to meet new people later. Here are just a few examples to get you started:

- Family members
- Friends—open your cell phone! One of the things people overlook (because it is with them every day) is their cell phone.
- Co-workers
- People you do business with, for example...insurance agents, landscaper, real estate agents, chiropractor, hairdresser, nail tech, pest control, veterinarian, home maintenance, massage therapist, day care provider
- People you know from church
- People you know from special interest groups (example: PTA)
- Business contacts (clients, peers in your industry)
- Professional Association contacts
- Organizations you volunteer time with (United Way, hospitals, food banks, shelters)
- People you know from classes you take (Mommy & Me, cooking, exercise, seminars, workshops, school)

The best thing to do is to just get started. Make a list of ten people who you know will love your product and who will be willing to listen and give you feedback on your presentation. The more you share your products with others, the more comfortable you will be.

PEOPLE YOU DON'T KNOW—YET (YOUR "COLD" MARKET)

In addition to the 200-plus people you already know, you also meet hundreds—even thousands—of people in your daily life. Do you talk to your grocery store clerk? To the other moms at the park? To your waitress? To your cab driver? Think of each of these people as a new relationship—and potential business partner. Here are some examples.

- People you meet while you are out in everyday life (where you work, grocery or department store, coffee shop, picking up your children from school, sport events)
- Referrals from friends/family/co-workers/current customers

We have seen this happen quite often: Someone on our team is looking to meet the CEO of a company or the decision-maker of a key account, and their best friend goes to lunch with that same person every week. Never underestimate the power of your sphere of influence and who they know, but the key is you must ASK and be specific as possible. Our brains respond better to recalling information when asked for specific information versus a general question.

Join your local Chamber of Commerce and go to their mixers—you will find many chapters within cities. Local business owners join, and there are often benefits like special "speed networking" events. Go as a guest first to their events and find the members who are positive and motivated about growing their business. Focus on meeting a few new members at each event and developing relationships with them over time. This is the heart of filling your tank.

Join BNI (Business Networking International), the largest business networking group in the world (www.bni.com). The format is standardized, regardless of whether you walk into a meeting in England or Arizona. Each person gets 60 seconds in front of the group to talk about his/her business. After these presentations are done, there will be one to two business owners who will get an in-depth 10 to 15 minutes to showcase their business. The goal of the group is for members to exchange referrals to each other's businesses, which makes it an excellent place to make new connections and introduce your business.

In any given city, there are many networking groups you can join to meet people. If your product/service is targeted toward a female audience, or you feel more comfortable at a women's-only group, here are a few suggestions to get you started:

National Association of Women Business Owners (NAWBO), www.nawbo.org. There are chapters all over the U.S. This group attracts women business owners with a luncheon format. In some chapters, you can purchase a table to showcase your product/service before and after the luncheon for a nominal fee. There is a featured speaker on various topics, and you will be able to introduce yourself around your lunch table and exchange business cards. This is another ideal way to get the word out about your product and start new relationships.

American Business Women's Association (ABWA), www.abwa.org. There are two types of formats for their meetings—an express luncheon and a dinner meeting. We recommend the Express Luncheon because the women drawn to these are more business-oriented; the dinner format is more social and less about business being conducted.

HeartLink Network (HLN), www.theheartlinknetwork.com. This is a great format. Meetings are informal, often conducted in women's homes, and dinner is included. You get three minutes in front of the group to talk about your business, but it is done in a very relaxed manner—no pressure! Emphasis is on connecting with other women and creating lasting relationships.

eWomen (www.ewomennetwork.com). This group attracts professional business women and uses the luncheon model. This group has a more formal format and an educational speaker, as well as structured networking exercises, which provide a great introduction to other business women.

When you are deciding to join any networking group, here are some tips to use in evaluating what will be a good fit for you:

- What is the energy of the group when you first walk in? Are they warm and inviting or standoffish or competitive?
- What is the cost of membership (joining fee, monthly dues, or the cost of a monthly breakfast/lunch/dinner)?

- Is your product/service a good compliment to the other businesses?
- Are you willing to commit to at least one year of attending the meetings consistently? Remember, trust and rapport are built over time, and people will do business with you when they feel comfortable that you will be there as the contact person. We have seen new people make the mistake of hopping from one group to another collecting business cards and thinking they will grow their business this way. People value relationships above all else!

Consider having a booth at a tradeshow or expo. Find out what local entrepreneurial events are coming up in your town. You can call your Chamber of Commerce or use Google to look up the calendar of events at your local convention center. This is best when you have one to three team members who can go with you to help you represent your company, so you can share expenses, support each other, and create teamwork.

Tips to think about:
- What is the cost?
- How many hours/days do you have to display your product/service?
- Who is the target market this tradeshow/expo will attract?
- Did the event planners do a good job with publicity?
- Is there only one booth allowed per company?
- How many sales will you need to make to break even and then profit, based on how much the booth cost?

If this is a local church expo, for example, the cost may be low, but most people are with their families and are focused on going to hear the pastor speak; they are not necessarily in a mindset that will be open to hearing about your product/service as they walk by. The key is to put yourself in the mindset of the people walking by your booth and ask yourself if this is an appropriate fit for the cost, time, and effort. It could be a home run or a total disappointment.

On a regional level, if you are a member of a professional association, consider having a booth at their regional or national conference. Again, this is best done with one to three team members.

Locally, here are a few ideas of associations you can be a part of in your area:

- Toastmasters
- Kiwanis
- Rotary
- Junior Achievement
- Small Business Association
- Photographer's Association
- Professional Organizers Association
- Event Organizers Association
- YWCA USA (Young Women's Christian Association USA)

One resource has a comprehensive list you can pay for to have access to professional and nonprofit associations, including up-to-date contact information: www.marketingsource.com

If you are already plugged into a network of any kind, create ways to meet and get to know more people in your network. For example, you might invite people one at a time to meet you over coffee or lunch, allowing you to build a one-to-one relationship and eventually do business together.

Host a get-together (or party) in your home or at a local restaurant and invite people so you can introduce them to your business in a relaxed, informal atmosphere.

If you are comfortable with a computer and navigating online and want to build your business using the Internet, join online networking groups such as Facebook, LinkedIn, and Twitter. Meetup.com is another great resource; you can find any group in your area, according to shared interests. Type in your zip code or topic of interest and it will list all of the groups near you that you can join. This site will even let you create your own group based on your interests and then people will find you.

What is your niche market? You already have a built-in network of people to talk to, based on your life experience. Think about your current career, evaluate your strengths, and go play in your sandbox. What does that mean? For example, you may be a dental hygienist. You already know the terminology used in your industry, which will help you to establish trust and rapport with other hygienists, and now you just add to the conversation about your product and service. Maybe your niche market is talking to high-income women business owners. Focus on that and become the expert known in that niche. One of the foremost experts in teaching people about marketing to affluent women is Annette Bau (founder www.millionaireseries.com).

What are your hobbies? Your hobbies will automatically draw you to others who share the same passion, which again helps you establish trust and rapport. This is an excellent way to meet others and strike up a natural conversation.

Bottom line—the more "strangers" you can turn into friends, the more success you will have in life and in your business. This last group of 12 ways to meet people will most likely challenge you to get out of your comfort zone by connecting with people you don't know. This may cause you some anxiety at first, so remember your *why*, step through your fear, and just try it! One of the things Kristi does before walking into a networking event is to take a couple of minutes to ask God (or a Higher power you believe in) for divine connections on who she is supposed to meet that day. That alleviates any pressure about needing to go around the room and gather up everyone's business card, and frees her to relax and enjoy the quality conversations and make new friends.

Be creative in turning a "cold" contact into a "warm" contact by developing the relationship with them whether in person, online, or on the phone. People do business with those they know, like, and trust! You will be amazed at the lifelong friendships you will create and the satisfaction you will feel in knowing you made a difference in people's lives with your product and your business opportunity.

With the down economy, now more than ever people are looking and praying for a solution. You could be it! Don't ever pre-judge, just consistently develop relationships and present your opportunity to others. You will be amazed at the results!

THINK IT OVER...

Take five minutes and make a list of your Warm Market here. Remember to simply write down everyone you think of without pre-judgment and without stopping. When the five minutes are up, circle the ten people you think are most likely to love your product and who you feel most comfortable with. Remember, successful network marketers constantly update, revise and add new names to their list, so schedule time once a month to do this exercise.

CHAPTER 8

Step on the Gas!

Now that you have met people using some of the ideas in the previous chapter, it is time to pull out of the driveway and on the road to your success! The following ideas and techniques will shave months off your learning curve, and help increase your *earning* curve. Before we begin, we would like to clarify the information we are about to share with you in this chapter. In network marketing you will hear quite often, "We **share** our product or service, we do not **sell**." Most people have a negative impression about selling, because they have had a bad experience (like having their driver's license held hostage at a car dealership so they can pressure you to sign a contract). When asked, most people would say people in sales are pushy, and not to be trusted. If this is your personal belief, then we are here to suggest it is possible to share the product or service you love and believe in AND also learn some sales skills that will help you be successful, while you remain true to yourself and keep your friends!

Sales = Service. When you approach each appointment by thinking "How can I best serve this person (in their personal life or business), then it will shift your paradigm and how you build your business. People will sense that you are being authentic and be attracted to your energy. Let's get started!

WHAT DO I SAY?

One of the most effective ways you can start a conversation is to take the pressure and focus off yourself and get to know the other person using the F.O.R.M. technique. It stands for Family, Occupation, Recreation, and Motivation/Money. Your goal is to find out about the other person using these ideas as starting points. This is not an "interrogation" where you are peppering questions at a stranger. Use a couple from each section, show genuine interest by listening to the responses and getting to know the person, and the conversation should flow easily from one topic to the next.

Do not make the mistake of trying to talk all about yourself or give a full-blown presentation to someone about your company, opportunity, product or service. When you meet someone, be there to meet them and exchange contact information; set up a separate time to get together to learn about each other's businesses.

Imagine meeting one of your friends for coffee—the minute you sit down you both are excited to find out what each other has been up to since the last time you met; this is the kind of energy you want to have.

Here are some opening questions in each of the four categories to help you get started:

Family & friends
Did you grow up here in (insert your state)?
Are you married?
Do you have any kids?
Do you have any pets? What kind?
Did you like growing up in the city/country?
Do your parents still live there?
Do you keep in touch with any childhood/college
   friends?

Occupation
What kind of work do you do?
What do you like about your job?
What's the most challenging thing about your job?
Do you like your boss/coworkers?
Is this your dream job and if not, what is?
Why did you choose this profession or how did you
   fall into this career?
What's the worst job you've ever had? What made it
   the worst?

Recreation
What do you like to do for fun?
What would you do if you had the whole day to your
   self?
How do you like to unwind after a long day?
What's your favorite type of food?
Do you like to play any sports?

What kind of music do you like?
Do you like to travel?
What is your favorite place?

Motivation/Money
What are you passionate about?
How did you get into that?
When you were a child what did you want to be
    when you grew up?
If you didn't have to work, what would you do with
    all your time?
Are you open to having residual income to help pay
    for (your home, car, vacation?)

Meeting with a new prospect can be exciting because of his or her life experiences, business background, children, and trips to other countries he or she has taken. Remember a road trip you may have taken as a child? Was it fun because there were other children in the car playing games and laughing with you to pass the time? One of the richest rewards in our industry is the people we meet and the lifelong friends we make. In the very near future you will look back and be surprised at how making the choice of owning your own business has added so many positive aspects to your journey. Have **fun!** As a side note, Kristi recently taught her eight-year-old daughter the F.O.R.M technique over breakfast, because Jade tends to be a little shy in social situations. In the car on the way to school, Jade shared that one of her friends incessantly talks about her family's ancestry, so Kristi suggested she use F.O.R.M. questions to find out other facts about her friend—problem solved! This can be used in everyday situations with any person you have a relationship with, so don't limit yourself to using it just for business contacts.

THE SALES MOUNTAIN

One of the master sales trainers in the world is our personal mentor of several years, Eric Lofholm (www. ericlofholm.com). He was mentored by and eventually became business partners with Donald Moine, PhD, who is one of the experts in the field of sales and marketing psychology. He also was a top producer for acclaimed national speaker Tony Robbins, and when he started his own sales coaching business 15 years ago, Robbins hired Lofholm back to train his sales staff.

Lofholm created the Sales Mountain, which is a culmination of 14 years of perfecting a systematic, step-by-step approach to sales. If it's done in a logical order, this system will help you have more success building your business. We have used this training with our teams, and people who never had any sales background start having better results. Why? Because once you understand that you don't have to be naturally gifted with sales skills, and that selling can be learned and duplicated by you and your team, you can take the pressure off yourself. Remember, you are just sharing a product or service that you love—but there is a process to doing it that will bring you more results when followed. This is the Sales Mountain.

Lofholm teaches us first to understand that selling equals service. Selling is about leading—moving people to action. Selling, influence, and persuasion are learned skills. Your prospect is silently begging to be led because you have a product/service that they need, and you are the one perceived as the expert.

Sales
MOUNTAIN

6. CLOSE ←——→ **7.** OBJECTION

SWEET SPOT
TOP 25%

5. SHARED BENEFITS   **8.** FOLLOW UP

4. ASSESSING NEEDS

3. TRUST & RAPPORT

2. APPOINTMENT SETTING

1. LEAD GENERATION   **9.** REFERRALS

Add value to your customer and always approach people with honor and integrity. The diagram shown on the previous page illustrates Lofholm's Sales Mountain. If you imagine approaching a new prospect starting on the left side of the mountain, and you follow each of these steps in order, without skipping a step, you will be able to achieve more success. This technique actually mimics the natural progression of how a relationship is established—if you try to skip a step, your prospect will feel uncomfortable and will keep his or her psychological guard up against you. It will be much harder to ask for the order and be successful in closing the sale.

1. Lead generation: The purpose of generating a lead is simply to gather more contacts. This is where using the "F.O.R.M" questions help you get to know your prospect—make sure you immediately add each person to your database.

2. Appointment setting: The purpose of calling is simply to make the appointment to share your product or business opportunity. Once the appointment is made, politely end the call. Although you may be excited to share your product or service right then, this is not the time to deliver your presentation. Many new people make this mistake, and then your prospect thinks he or she has enough information to make a decision, when in reality, they don't.

3. Trust/rapport: This step is critical—find common ground and develop a rapport with your prospect. Do not skip this step! Imagine going on a first date with someone and, five minutes into dinner, your date declares, "I am in love with you. Will you marry me?" Most people would react by thinking, "Stalker! I need to change my phone number!" If, however, the appropriate amount of time passes for the couple to get to know each other, develop rapport, and they mutually fall in love, asking the same question would have a much different reaction. It is the same in the sales process; people want to know you care about them before you tell them all about you, your product, and your opportunity.

Note: Within this section you can use a system to help you develop trust and rapport. Everyone has one of four different communication styles (we appreciate learning this information from Tom "Big Al" Schreiter, www.fortunenow.com, "The Secret Language of Prospects"). Read these four color descriptions and identify what your personal style is, and then practice using this with everyone you meet so you will in minutes be able to talk to your prospect in their language. If you were to travel to a foreign country, and took the time to learn a few key words or phrases to get around, it would be easier and more enjoyable to connect with people; using these key phrases will help you connect with your prospect and create positive results.

YELLOW COMMUNICATION STYLE:

Identify: Huggers. They like eco-friendly products. They will put others' needs before their own. They are not motivated by money. Likeable, loveable, kind. They will start talking about you before they talk about themselves. Clothes: Cottons or comfortable clothes, sensible shoes, little/no makeup, not flashy. Occupations: Professional helper, fundraising, volunteer, massage therapist, health care, ministry, psychologist, school teacher. How to invite them to an event: "I need your help bringing ice/greeting people at the door to make them feel comfortable/helping to set up/clean up—can I count on you?" What turns them off? Talking about compensation plans, the business opportunity, direct eye contact; don't start off a meeting with them by jumping right in to your presentation.

Negative side: They are wishy-washy, base their opinions on what others think, and don't like being at the front of the room doing presentations. Key words to their language: help, love, security, friends.

BLUE COMMUNICATION STYLE:

Identify: People-oriented, center of attention, visionary/big picture people, great motivators, great prospectors and promoters. Clothes: Colorful, hip/trendy, make-up/hair/nails are important to them, great shoes are must! Occupations: Sales, travel agents, tour guides, entrepreneurs. How to invite them to an event: "I am so excited for you to come to the event! There will be so many fun people I want to introduce you to! You can win trips with our company!

Negative side: They are usually late. They are non-stop talkers (during movies, presentations, answer their own questions), easily distracted, don't follow up with people, it's hard for them to stay focused. Key words to their language: people, fun, party, vacations.

RED COMMUNICATION STYLE:

Identify: Like to be in charge, control freaks, great organizers, like to be at the front of the room doing presentations, like to be recognized, competitive. They will use brief answers when talking with you. Clothes: Quality suits/dresses and shoes. They like to look good before going out in public (they also like nice cars, anything that will make their "image" look good). Occupations: CEO's, managers, sales, business owners. How to invite them to an event: Talk to them in bullet points. "Come to the event so I can introduce you to some of the top people in our company." What turns them off? People who don't make eye contact, talk too much, and don't have confidence when approaching them.

Negative side: Headstrong, judgmental, competitive, think they know everything, they will interrupt you while you're talking. They will make up their minds in the first one to three minutes of your presentation whether they will do business with you. Key words to their language: money, recognition, power, win.

GREEN COMMUNICATION STYLE:

Identify: Technical, analytical, detail-oriented, linear thinkers, organizers. Clothes: Conservatively dressed, no flashy colors. Occupations: Technical fields, quality control, bookkeepers, tax accountant. How to invite them to an event: "There's a lot of great information that will be shared and you will want to take notes." What turns them off? Being kept waiting, making up answers.

Negative side: They will want to read and research everything to make sure they are making the "right" decision (analysis paralysis). Key words to their language: data, facts, research, information.

4. Assessing needs: Ask your prospect questions to find out what he or she is doing to grow his or her business, achieve better health, create more income, etc. Listen and assess if your product or service can help this person. Remember, your goal is to help others. You may find out they are satisfied with the way things are in their personal, financial, spiritual, or business aspects of their life. If that is the case, then you can go right to step nine and ask for referrals. If not, proceed to step five.

5. Shared benefits: Describe how your product or service can help generate more business for your prospect, help them create better health, save them time and money, etc. Share with the person how you can help her. Focus on her needs, not yours.

6. Close: Once you have followed steps one through 5, you are now at the peak of the Sales Mountain, or "sweet spot." Ask for the order, and then be silent. Most people fail at this step. They do not ask for the order, or, if they do, they do not remain silent for the prospect to answer. You will notice there is an arrow going back and forth between step 6 and 7—this is where you "elegantly dance" with your prospect. If he or she gives you an objection, ask a specific question to understand the reason for the objection. Then solve the problem, ask for the order again, and remain silent. Once you are in this sweet spot with the prospect, you are at the point where it is easier to move him/her to action.

7. Objection Handling: Most people, especially women, have trouble with this step because they are afraid of being rejected, or because they don't know how to respond to an objection effectively. If you approach this like you're a detective trying to uncover how you can help solve your prospect's needs, then it isn't as scary. Know that usually the first objection isn't the true reason they are saying "no." The prospect is trying to buy some time before they make a decision. An objection is just a question that your prospect has that you didn't cover during your presentation. If your prospect does say "no," it does not mean forever; it just means for that moment in time it isn't right for them. Here is the great news: In the network marketing industry, no matter what product or service you represent, there are only a handful of objections you will hear. Some of them are:

   a. I don't have the money.
   b. I don't have the time.
   c. I need to check with my spouse/significant other.
   d. I need to think about it.
   e. I need more information.
   f. I already tried something similar and it didn't work.
   g. I'm not interested.

Techniques for your tool kit:

Here are several different techniques to address these objections:

Story: One of the most powerful ways to handle an objection is with a story. The reason stories are so persuasive is that they act as invisible selling. Stories also suspend time. Identify true stories that address the prospect's situation. One way to start off the story is by saying, "That reminds me of a story of a client who was in a similar situation. Let me share with you what they did..."

Question: You can answer an objection with a question. For example:

Objection: "The price is too high"
Response: "By too high, what exactly do you mean?"
Response: "How much is too much?"
Response: "Compared to what?"

Objection: "I don't have the time."
Response: "When will you have the time?"
Response: "On a scale of one to 10, how motivated are you to move forward?"
Response: "What do you mean by that?"

Isolate: Isolating an objection is a favorite technique. because it is very effective and easy to learn.

Objection: "I don't have the money."
Response: "I can appreciate that. Other than the money, is there anything else that is preventing you from taking action today?" Be silent and listen for their answer.

Objection: "I don't have the time."
Response: "Other than the time, is there anything else preventing you from moving forward today?" Be silent.

Investigate: "Tell me more about that." Listen to what your prospect is saying and assess if you can help solve his/her problem.

Always be sensitive to your prospect's needs. There may be a lot of personal stuff going on in their life that has nothing to do with whether they will use your product or not. Remember a "no" today doesn't necessarily mean "NO" forever. Do not take a rejection/objection personally—it's all about timing.

I love your system, but I can't afford it right now.
Response: "I understand—other than the money, is there anything else keeping you from moving forward today?" Be quiet and let them answer. "When would it be okay for me to follow up with you?" Once the prospect gives you a date, make SURE to write it in your planner/Outlook calendar/Blackberry, etc. and **call her back!**

8. Follow Up: If your prospect chooses not to get started, they fall below the sweet spot, and now you are headed down the right side of the Sales Mountain. Once this happens, it is harder to re-create the same excitement the person had when you first did the presentation. The key here is to be consistent with your follow-up. Ask if you can follow up in a week. Then agree on a date and time, write it down, and make sure you follow through. Our industry standard is most customers will not move to action until you have contacted them five to seven times (phone/email/card/text). However, most people give up after the first or second follow up, and your prospect will most likely sign up with someone else who does follow up multiple times!

9. Referrals: Always ask for referrals, and find ways to refer business to your prospect to help build his or her business if they have one. Be specific in the type of referral you are looking for: "Who do you know who is a chiropractor/insurance agent/real estate agent?" It is easier for people to recall someone's name quickly from their memory when you give a specific request than if you say, "I am looking for people who want to be healthy."

Once you understand the Sales Mountain and practice it until it becomes an automatic part of your process for meeting with prospects, the following ideas will help you hone your skills and build your team.

DEVELOP YOUR 60-SECOND COMMERCIAL

Create a concise, easy-to-understand 60-second "commercial" or "interest-creating remark" to have ready at a moment's notice. When someone asks, "What do you do?" you will be able to tell the person in 60 seconds what your product or service is, with the end result being that they will want to reconnect with you to find out more.

An example of how you can share what you do is using a simple script for your commercial. "I help people in (the prospect's industry) with (state the benefit of your product/service)." This is easy to remember, and it immediately creates curiosity with your prospect because you are appealing to the question in their mind, "what's in it for me?" This is also simple enough to teach your team how to effectively duplicate what you did.

APPOINTMENT-SETTING

Some people will have no problem setting appointments; others may find this part a challenge because they fear rejection. When you are asking someone for an appointment, do not make the mistake of trying to give your entire presentation to them right then and there. Set the appointment and then be courteous and end the phone call, or, if in person, end the conversation about your business and switch the topic to something else.

You can spot a novice in a room full of people because they are the ones who are thrusting a business card at someone, then a DVD, then a brochure, and then inviting their prospect to a presentation. By this time, the prospect has the "Where's the exit?" look on their face and will try to get away from the person as fast as possible. The novice will then wonder why people will not return calls—ever. Be professional, courteous, and well-mannered—these attributes go a long way with people remembering you in a positive way.

An example of a simple phone script to use may be "Hi, this is (your name) from (your company). We met at (event). Did I catch you at a good time?" The reason it is good business practice to ask that question is because if the person is running out the door or has a sick child, it's best to ask when a better day/time to call back would be. If you get a positive response, then you can say, "You had expressed interest in wanting to know more about our (your product/service). Are you available either Tuesday or Thursday, at (state time)?" Agree on the day/time, and then, as stated above, end the phone call courteously. Make sure to write the appointment down and follow up.

THE BUSINESS PRESENTATION

When you first start sharing your product, service or business opportunity with people, make sure you are inviting your sponsor to be with you in person or on a three-way call. If your company uses the home party model, allow your sponsor to act as host for you until you feel more comfortable.

It is important to use "edification"—the art of introducing your prospect to your sponsor and your sponsor to your prospect in such a way that you are complimenting both to each other. Highlight each person's skills, accomplishments, or qualities. This helps bring credibility to your company, to yourself, and to your prospect. Then step back and let your sponsor walk through the first few presentations.

Once you feel comfortable, have your sponsor be there for support as you gradually take over the driver's seat. This is key for your success because you will be able to take notes on the questions being asked and how they are answered. This is also indirectly training your prospect, should he or she decide to join your team, because they get to see the process in action.

Guess what? You will make mistakes. You will not know all of the answers. If you've ever learned to drive a stick shift car, do you remember what that was like? Grinding gears, popping the clutch, the terror of having to stop on a hill and trying not to roll backwards when the light turned green, while drivers behind you grew impatient or tried to back up so they wouldn't get hit? Little by little, it got easier—and, today, you would be able to do it without thinking. This is the learning process for anything new. Recognize your fear as just part of the process, put the key in, step on the gas, and get started anyway.

FOLLOW UP, FOLLOW UP, FOLLOW UP

One of the keys to building a successful business is having a follow-up system that you do consistently. Many, many sales are left on the table because the person fails to call, email, or send a card after the first meeting or after the presentation. Or, the person stops calling after the first unanswered call, because she thinks it is a personal rejection, as opposed to a more likely story, which is that people are leading busy lives and fail to return calls. As we mentioned above, the industry standard is that it takes five to seven contacts before your prospect will move to action with you and get started.

To help you keep track of your follow-ups, create a tracking system you are comfortable using. It can be high tech, such as using an Excel Spreadsheet, Outlook task feature, Oprius.com, etc., or low tech, such as writing it on a yellow legal pad, using a day planner, or implementing a 31-day file system. There is no right or wrong way, as long as you are consistent and at a glance you know where you are with any given prospect. Some suggestions for your tracking sheet:

Name

Phone number

Where you met

Appointment set

Presentation done

Follow-up call (leave seven spaces for this section— note the date and time so if you are not reaching the prospect, you can see the pattern of what time of day has not worked so far, and then change your strategy. Try a different time of day or try reaching the prospect by email, sending a card, or texting.)

Date signed up as a customer or team builder

Training done (if applicable to your product or service); if they are a new team member, then you will train them on how to build their own business.

KEY POINT

Just because you hear "no" today does not mean it is a "no" forever. If the prospect agrees to you following up, put the future date in your tracking system and then be courteously persistent. For many people, timing is critical when they are ready to use your product/service—remember, this is part of keeping your tank full. In Kristi's case, when she first was introduced to her current company, she said, "I would never use your product and service." Two short months later, as she shared in Chapter 5, circumstances changed, she reconnected with the person, and she now has a huge team growing every month.

KAREN'S STORY:

After moving to Texas, I took out all of my old contacts—two years' worth of business cards and contact forms! I went through each contact one by one, calling them just to let them know I had moved and to see if they were still interested in my product. These were people I had followed up with consistently over the years, but had not heard from for a long time. As I was leaving my phone number for one woman I had met a year earlier, I got cut off, so I called back to leave my number. This time she answered! When I told her who I was, she got so excited! "Someone just showed me this, but I could never go with anyone else after all the follow-up you have done! I'm ready to get started, let's make an appointment for next week." Not only did I get a new customer, but I inspired someone to do better at her own follow-up! The moral of the story? You never know! Just keep following up until the person tells you to stop.

USE YOUR COMPANY'S TOOLS

Every company has marketing tools that have been carefully researched to be the most effective at selling your product or service and introducing your company's business opportunity. These tools include CDs, DVDs, magazines, brochures, product samples, and many more. Use them!

Most importantly, be a product of the product. If you are in a health and wellness company, make sure you are using the product so you can have your own personal story to share. If you are in a beauty products company, then your face is your biggest asset in selling your products. You must be authentic and have integrity—people can sense it immediately if you do not. They may never say it out loud; they just will not return your calls and will align with someone else who they resonate with better.

TRAIN YOUR NEW TEAM MEMBER

In your company, there will be an established system and checklist of how to properly train your new team member. First of all, make sure you are following the system, become comfortable at it, and then teach it to your team. Educate about the basics of network marketing—it is a three- to five-year commitment before your new business partner will start to see significant, life-changing paychecks. You never know who will be your next business builder who will go on to lead a huge team—so your job is to just get someone started. Do not build someone's team for them; teach them how to do it themselves, or else you will have a weak team that will eventually diminish.

Keep in mind too, that training is an ongoing process for everyone who chooses to be successful in network marketing. After you do the initial training with your new team member, it is her responsibility to take it from there. Make yourself available for questions and ongoing support and point them to the ongoing training resources available locally and through the company, but your basic training job with them is done.

THINK IT OVER...

Take a moment to examine your old ideas about "selling." If they are negative feelings about selling, shift your mindset to, "How can I serve this person and what are the benefits of my product or service for them?"

Did you know that "sales" is a learned skill? Write down an accountability partner who you can practice the Sales Mountain process with—someone who can give you gentle feedback.

In looking at the four color personality styles, which one do you relate to most? How can you utilize this knowledge to communicate better with your family, friends and people you meet?

Who can you practice F.O.R.M with?

Brainstorm some ideas for your 60-second commercial. Think "value/benefit," and keep it concise. Practice it out loud until you can say it without hesitation.

CHAPTER 9

Lead a Caravan

One of the greatest aspects of network marketing is the *network!* As you bring new people into your business, you're building a team of networkers who are helping you to grow your business, even as they grow their own businesses. As you progress in your business and become a team leader, there are some important things to remember that will help you grow your team and lead them to their dreams while you are reaching yours.

DUPLICATION IS VITAL TO YOUR SUCCESS

One of the best features of the network marketing business model is that you do NOT have to be a great salesperson to be successful! This is not about you getting thousands of customers to use your product/service.

The successful network marketer only needs to find a few people who want to use the product and find a few who also want to build a business with you—and teach them **how to do exactly what you do.**

KEY POINT

Once you get a few others started, it's not just about you anymore. You never stop sponsoring new people, but your focus needs to be on team-building and helping others duplicate your success. Learning how to teach others to duplicate what has worked for you is the key to massive growth and success in our type of business.

Here are some tips that can make all the difference:

- Have a system for getting someone started
- Keep it simple—don't get fancy
- Teach it consistently

Many people who start a network marketing team make the mistake of not teaching an easily duplicatable system, or they will jump from idea to new idea on how to train their team. Then, in the eternal quest to find the "perfect" system or a "short cut," the team will become confused and growth will slow down as the team members get bogged down in learning the details of each new way.

Invariably, you will be excited about starting your own business; resist the urge to come up with new and creative ideas on how to get started. You will lose precious time and momentum trying to re-invent your company's system instead of using tried and true methods from the top income earners. Once you have mastered your company's process, then you can tailor it slightly for your personality.

One of the most successful and respected people in network marketing today, Jordan Adler, wisely states, "If an eight-year-old cannot follow what you are doing, then it's too difficult...simple is key!" The bottom line is to know your product/service, learn the easiest way to teach others, and do not deviate from that same message, no matter what others are doing around you.

LEADERSHIP

Once you have a few others sharing your product and your message, you have a team, and you have moved into a position of leadership since they are looking to you for guidance. Always keep in mind that your team will do what you do, so pay attention to your own thoughts, words, and actions!

There are several ways you can be a leader. You may be comfortable standing at the front of the room conducting monthly trainings—but if you are not, that's okay. There are very powerful leaders who grow their teams one by one, sitting across the table from people in their homes. There are still others who have little personal contact with their team members, but lead by means of conference calls, e-mails, and webinars.

The "how" is individual, but the "what" includes these ten leadership principles:

- Be a self-starter—don't wait to always be told what to do.
- Lead by example—do yourself what you want your team to do. They are watching your actions more than your words.
- Encourage each new distributor to believe in himself/herself.
- Provide inspiration and vision for your team.
- Teach the skills and system that your reps need to succeed.
- Stay positive always.
- Take responsibility. Don't blame or be a victim.

- Don't let challenges stop you.
- Recognize the efforts and promotions of team members.
- Respect others always, and have an attitude of gratitude.

The important thing is to be aware of your own mindset and energy and to be courageous enough to work on yourself and make changes if necessary. Stepping into your greatness as a leader is more internal than external—the more you develop your own skills and mindset, the more you will have to share with your team. Always be in the process of personal growth and becoming better. True leaders never feel that they know it all; they are perpetual students of growth.

TEAM-BUILDING
First team-building goal:
When you first start building your business, it will often feel like you are working hard, and you are building your team single-handedly. Our best advice is to set a goal in your first year of personally signing up (sponsoring) 24 to 30 business builders yourself, approximately two to three per month. Statistically, one of that group of 24 will take off and build a huge team under you, but at the outset you won't know which one is going to be that superstar. So make it a goal to just sign up your 24 to 30. Remember not to pre-judge. There is an old saying in our industry, "the one you think will (be a superstar) won't, and the ones you think won't, will!"

Once you have around 24 to 30 people signed up on your team, the focus becomes teaching them to be able to duplicate at least three levels down. A "leg" that has duplicated down three levels is considered to be secure and will then continue to grow on its own without your guidance. Think of your business as a tree developing a strong root system that grows automatically over time. A tree with strong roots won't blow over in a storm and will result in a healthy tree that will thrive for years to come.

Getting to 100:

Once you get your first 24 to 30 distributors started on your team, your next goal is to grow that number (including everyone in all your "legs") to 100 as quickly as possible. The reason is this: It can often seem like it takes forever to build that first group of 100, but, once you have achieved that first 100 mark, you will then ex-perience faster geometric team growth. As more people from this group of 100 sponsor their own new distribu-tors, the team will double to 200 in a fraction of the time it took to build the initial group. Every subsequent group of 100 new distributors happens quicker than the last, and soon your team will be doubling in size every few months—and you'll know it was worth the wait!

Become a leader of leaders:

Once the top achievers on your team start to emerge, it is time to help them become leaders of their own teams. This is how you duplicate yourself so you can move on to find new business builders without having to manage everyone on your growing team personally. If you do not do this, you will burn out! If you do, your team can grow to unlimited heights and you will still have the energy to enjoy the process.

Learn to be aware of your up-and-coming leaders' personal behavioral styles and strengths, and then help them to refine and expand their skills. It will always be about people skills and the relationships they build first and the product second, which goes back to the importance of ongoing training and personal growth.

Teach your new leaders to honor others and to respect the differences in personalities, customs, beliefs, and individual styles. Encourage your leaders to read books by the classic personal growth authors like Earl Nightingale, Dale Carnegie, Jim Rohn, and Zig Ziglar. Having leadership retreats once or twice a year encourages future growth and replenishment of the body, mind, and spirit. Your company may provide them; if not, create your own.

Express encouragement and gratitude to your team regularly, which will help them to keep going on their own journeys to success in your business. Look for opportunities to recognize achievements, company promotions, and general excellence in your team members at all times. (Remember, some people work harder for recognition than for money!) And always be ready to help your teammates who ask for help. You could be the difference between them sticking with the journey long enough to be successful and achieving their dreams or dropping out too soon and failing. As Zig Ziglar says, "Help enough people get what they want and you will get what you want."

THINK IT OVER...

Who has been a significant leader for you in your life?

What characteristics do they have?

What leadership traits do you already have that can serve you in your new business?

CHAPTER 10

Getting Past Detours and Bumps in the Road: Dealing With Challenges

Question: What is the #1 reason why people fail in a network marketing business?

Answer: Because they quit too soon!

If you were on an important road trip from San Diego to New York, why would you quit and give up your journey when you only got as far as Omaha, Des Moines, or Pittsburgh? Why would someone stop and quit their business before reaching their goals and dreams? Because they fell prey to one or more detours on their journey. Be aware of these bumps in the road so they don't catch you off guard:

1) The bump in the road called "Disappointment," when someone says "no" to buying your product/service or joining your team as a distributor when you are certain they would benefit from it or be an awesome team builder.

2) The barrier called "Discouragement," when one of your new team members never even gets started (known as the perpetual "getting ready to get ready" syndrome).

3) The pothole called "Deception," when someone on your team promises to build a huge organization under you and then does nothing, or leaves your group for another company.

4) The detour of "Dismay," when some of your team members drop out only halfway through their own journey to financial freedom.

The reality is that many distributors will stop building their business in their first few months or years. Momentum doesn't happen overnight, and new reps without a strong *why* and a solid inner foundation may not make it. Every successful network marketer has had to deal with this reality. You can either use the high dropout factor as an excuse to quit yourself, or keep going on your own journey. The choice is totally yours.

As caring and compassionate women, we may also fall into the trap of trying to "carry" inactive team members on our backs as we journey down the road to freedom in a misguided effort to help them. This will only slow down your own business growth, and typically your efforts to carry others who are not working the business will not motivate them; it just makes them dependent on you. We strongly caution you not to confuse caring with "carrying"! To quote the great female network marketing pioneer Kim Klaver, "You can't drag others across the finish line."

PERSONAL COPING STRATEGIES

Here's how to cope with the detours and bumps in the road so you don't let the actions of others drag you down and put the enemy of doubt in your mind.

The Big Picture

To complete your journey and be successful, you must stay focused on the Big Picture—your *why*—and think long-term when negative situations arise. Disappointments are only temporary. Remember the deep emotional *why*, the dream that drove you to start your business. Revisit your Vision Board and refocus on your goals. Get support from your sponsor or other trusted leaders in your company. Stay focused on your Big Picture goals and dreams, and they will lead you like a shining beacon on the path to your greatness and your freedom.

Think Long-Term

Typically, thinking long-term in network marketing means only five to seven years! Could you keep going for five to seven years if you KNEW you would reach your destination and your dreams could come true in that timeframe?

There is an old saying in network marketing that is as true today as it will be years from now: "It's easy to pay the price when the promise is clear."

Here's the bottom line for getting to the finish line:

Once you have found the right product and company for you, MAKE A COM-MITMENT to yourself and your family that you will work your business for three to five years part-time or full-time NO MATTER WHAT.

Then **take action every day** to move your business forward. It doesn't need to be a lot of hours per day. Remember most people build their fortune part-time around their jobs, family, and other life commitments—but it does need to be **focused** and **consistent**. Starting and stopping will severely slow down your business growth or even kill it. Consistency of action is the key, and Big Picture thinking will keep you on the path and in the game until you reach your destination—FREEDOM!

STRATEGIES TO MINIMIZE TEAM ATTRITION

The truth is, it will likely take two to three years of consistent effort for a network marketer's residual income to replace his/her job income and a few more years after that for most to finance their goals and dreams. Many people in today's world simply do not have the discipline to consistently put in five to seven years of prospecting, sharing their product/service, sponsoring, and training. And sometimes "life" happens and things get in the way. Therefore, attrition is to be expected on your team and is part of the process of building it.

Here are four strategies to help minimize your team's attrition rate and keep them "in the game" until they have enough success to never want to quit:

- Work closely with new team members you sponsor in their first 30 days and help them have success right out of the gate. There is nothing like getting a check right away to keep a new person excited.

- Hold regular local team trainings and make socializing and networking a part of these events. Make your team members feel a sense of belonging to something bigger than themselves, and make it fun. Building relationships can do wonders for team longevity!

- Keep in touch regularly with your team through email and conference calls, especially as your team grows to places outside of your geographic area. Building long distance relationships is a critical skill if you want to create and maintain a big team.

- Most importantly, get your team to events as much as possible. This includes regional company events and especially the annual convention. The positive group energy at these gatherings will keep your team members enthusiastic and motivated to go home and work their business in a way that nothing else can. Become a promoter of these trainings and events, with the goal of keeping your team in the game until they have enough success to never want to quit.

AN IMPORTANT SECRET

Despite the above strategies, you will have team members who quit your business. Here's a secret many people new to network marketing don't know: The majority of your income from your team will be generated from only a few key people. These will be your "aces," the one in 24 to 30 previously mentioned who will build a huge team under you and create those "key legs" that will take your business toward your dreams. So don't spend sleepless nights over those that drop out—they were not your aces.

How do you know when you have an "ace" on your team?

1)   They take responsibility for learning how to do the business without waiting for you to do it for them.

2)   They take consistent action without needing to be pushed.

3)   They don't complain or quit over their own challenges.

4)   They show up to events and training calls.

5)   They build their own large group of distributors and become leaders—without you holding their hand along the way.

KEY POINT

Find five to ten of these "aces" and focus on encouraging them as leaders. Learn to let go of the rest because many of them will not make it to the finish line.

UNREALISTIC EXPECTATIONS

Question: What is another big reason people fail in network marketing?

Answer: Unrealistic expectations

Our society has taught us to expect instant results—the "just add water and stir mentality." Because of this, and because some network marketers have spread hype about what can be earned upfront in our profession, it is not uncommon to see new reps quit when they don't see huge checks in their first 90 days of being in business.

Here's another place to pause and take a long-term view:

If you had invested thousands of dollars in law school, how long would you expect to work before just breaking even? If you borrowed thousands of dollars to start a traditional business or franchise, would you expect to be in the profit zone immediately after opening your business? It would take years of hard work just to be in the black.

In the network marketing business model, the good news is that you can recoup your investment of a few hundred dollars or less in just a few weeks, as opposed to years. The bad news is that you will not typically see big dollars at first, relative to the time and effort you are putting into your new venture. If you have unrealistic expectations, you are traveling a slippery road.

KEY POINT

Do NOT look at your checks during your first six months and ask yourself, "Is it worth it?" Our business takes time. Again, keep your eyes on your why *and your goals. And remember Big Picture Thinking!*

Revisit this question after your network marketing business is one to two years old. By then the power of duplication and leveraging yourself should have kicked in, and you will know the answer to that question. If you have taken consistent action, you should have a growing business with checks coming in regularly and you won't need to ask yourself that question again.

By the end of year three, you should see major progress toward your goals and dreams as your checks increase to meet them and give them wings. By year five you should be closing in on your dreams. By years seven to ten, you should be FREE or close to it!

IS IT WORTH IT?

Where else can you invest a few hundred dollars, work part-time for five to ten years, and then be financially free with income coming to you automatically each month? Ask any network marketer who has survived the disappointments, detours, and bumps in the road to reach their dreams—it is so worth it!

They all were able to reach their destination through consistent effort, thinking long term, having faith, patience, getting support from their team and their families, and having fun along the way, sharing a product or service they love and helping others to achieve their dreams too. Network marketing can be the most rewarding journey you will ever take!

NETWORK MARKETING AND THE SNOWBALL

What if you got paid to push a big snowball over a mountain? Have you ever tried to push a snowball uphill? At first, it feels like you are the only one pushing. After awhile, a couple people join you and start helping you push. It's still hard, but not as lonely.

A bit later, there are a few more people pushing the snowball, and, even though it is growing, the load feels lighter because you are now part of a team. You are all working together for a common purpose.

After more time elapses, you see that you are closer to the top of the mountain. You look around and realize that your team has doubled and tripled since you last counted, as they have themselves found more people to join the group effort.

At last you reach the top and find that you don't have to push the snowball uphill anymore. In fact, it is poised to start rolling down the other side of the mountain and you get ready for that. The snowball starts down, gathers momentum, then a lot of momentum. As it goes faster and faster downhill, you have all you can do to hang on for the ride of your life.

THAT is the journey of network marketing!

SUGGESTED TIMELINE FOR YOUR JOURNEY TO FREEDOM

30 days—At first, it's just you presenting your product/service to people in your network. You don't have a team yet and you aren't making much income. You are working part-time around your regular job.

30 to 90 days—You have signed up a few customers and a couple of other business builders to start your team. It feels good not to be alone any longer, but you still aren't seeing much income.

90 to 180 days—Your team is growing, but not fast. You see a slight rise in your income when you get your first promotion, but not enough to justify the hours you are putting into your business. This is a "danger zone" where many people quit.

180 days to one year—Your team has doubled and you earned a second promotion. Your checks are going up, but not enough to equal your job salary, so you need to keep working plus continue doing your business part time. You may wonder if it's worth it—danger zone!

18 months to two years—Your team has tripled and you earned your third promotion. Your residual income check has a comma in it! Your team has grown and spread out to include many states. You decide it IS worth it and keep going. You are past the biggest danger zone.

Three years—You have now equaled your salary. You can quit your job if you choose and go full-time doing what you love. You are well on your way to time and financial freedom, but you still need to work the business daily.

Five years—Your residual income has doubled and tripled. Your bills are paid. You have extra to save every month toward your dream home or dream car, and you can take the dream vacation with your family.

Five to ten years—You are now financially free with thousands in monthly residual income for life, even if you stop working. Congratulations—you did it!

THINK IT OVER...

Would you quit if someone says "no" to your product or business? How about five people? What about ten to 20? How many "no's" would you accept before you quit?

What if your good friend asks you to build her business for her? Would you "carry" her?

List two to three personal coping strategies for dealing with the challenges you are likely to face.

List some fun things you can do with your team to create cohesion and minimize people dropping out.

Can you keep your eyes focused on your dream for three to five years until you arrive at your journey's end (financial freedom)?

CONCLUSION

Network marketing at its best is not a get rich quick scheme. It's a journey of personal development toward a lifestyle of time and financial freedom that many simply cannot imagine. As you read in the previous chapters, becoming a successful entrepreneur is a matter of dreaming big and sticking to it. The three of us have all had our moments of doubt. We have watched as some soared, and others quit. The difference between the two had nothing to do with the number of connections or the person's sales training or personality. It had to do with their determination to succeed.

Is your *why* big enough? We recently heard a story from one of our favorite people, Jordan Adler, that illustrates this point. Imagine that you are at the top of a skyscraper in the middle of a snowstorm. Stretching out in front of you is a thin, slippery, rail-less bridge across the city. Would you cross the bridge for $100? $1,000? A million dollars? Remember—this slippery, thin bridge is hundreds of feet above the city. The wind and snow are swirling around you. Now, imagine that your child is at the other end of that bridge waiting to be rescued. Would you even hesitate? No matter the obstacles, you would get to your baby. And if your *why* is big enough and real enough to you, you will make it through all the obstacles. You will keep going, because in the end you know it will all be worth it.

KAREN'S STORY

My family and I recently moved from Arizona to Texas. My husband Ryan is a general contractor, and he wanted to pursue building opportunities in Texas. So, we loaded up our things and began the journey to the unknown, leaving all of our friends and family behind. Not even 15 miles out of our small Arizona town, Ryan's truck broke down and we had to be towed back, only to discover that the engine was ruined and would take weeks and thousands of dollars to fix. Trading in my car for a more reliable truck that would get us to Texas, we were back on our way. About 90 miles into the trip, just outside of Phoenix, we stopped for gas, only to discover that the tread on **all four** of the trailer's tires were losing their tread. Two hours and $500 later, we were on the road again.

Arriving in Texas, we discovered that a flood the week before had created a run on the rental market, as 100 families searched for temporary housing. As soon as we walked in the door of a potential property, we were told that the house was already rented. We finally found a house available a month later. Fortunately, we were able to stay with some friends of my husband's parents in their one bedroom, one bathroom casita. (Remember, we have three children, ages 3,5, and 8, and no toys, no TV!)

Finally, the big moving day arrived. We loaded up the kids and headed to our new home. Fifteen miles into the journey, Ryan saw something bouncing across the road in the rear-view mirror. Sure enough, we had completely lost the tire off the trailer. The wheel had broken completely off the axle.

So, late on a Sunday afternoon, we called around frantically searching for a U-Haul office that was open. We loaded up the kids, picked up the U-Haul, unpacked the trailer, loaded the U-Haul, and finally reached our destination late in the evening, exhausted but happy to finally be at the end of our journey.

A friend recently asked me, with all of THAT happening, how in the world did we know we were doing the right thing? In her words, "We pray about things and sometimes I think if things go smoothly then it was meant to be. When we hit a snag we don't push any further. I am just asking because of all the stuff that happened to try to keep you here. I am just wondering how you knew that this is what you're supposed to be doing?"

For me, the answer is that we knew *why* we were moving to Texas. We were sure that we were doing the right thing, and no obstacle in the world was going to stop us. Many times, just when we were about to give up hope, some little thing would show us that we were on the right track. Was our journey an easy one? NO! Was it worth it? YES! We are where we need to be because we didn't give up and we were sure of our destination.

YOUR WHY

As you build your network marketing business, remember your *why*. We can't say it enough! Remember how it felt to be a little girl—back when the sky was the limit. Back before the worries of life bogged you down... dream big! Let yourself soar in your imagination, and you will soar in your life. Take this License to Dream that we are giving you today and go for it!

The "Doubling Penny" Story

A wealthy father had twin teenage daughters, both of whom he thought were pretty darn sharp. One afternoon while he and his daughters were gathered around the kitchen table, the dad, always a firm believer in visualizing and working toward goals, decided to offer them both a month-long apprenticeship in his business so they'd have the opportunity to make enough cash to fully finance their dreams of attending major universities. In addition, dad thought his employment offer would be a great learning experience for them both.

"I've got a proposition for you, daughters! Work for me for one month in my business and I'll pay you either a cool $10,000 per day, or a single penny on day one and double your salary each day for 30 days. What do you say? Oh, and I'll give a $100,000 bonus to whomever makes the most money in total at the end of 30 days."

Daughter #1 immediately chose the $10,000 per day option, while daughter #2 decided to try something different and chose the "doubling penny" option.

Let's put the rest of the story on hold for a moment. Which payment option would YOU have chosen? $10,000 a day or the "doubling penny"? Clearly, $10,000 a day adds up to $300,000. Would you have chosen a guaranteed $300,000 or the unknown? Let's see if you would have made the right decision:

	$10,000/day			The "Doubling Penny"	
Day	**$ Paid**	**Total**		**$ Paid**	**Total**
1	$10,000	$10,000		$.01	$.01
2	$10,000	$20,000		$.02	$.03
3	$10,000	$30,000		$.04	$.07
4	$10,000	$40,000		$.08	$.15
5	$10,000	$50,000		$.16	$.31
6	$10,000	$60,000		$.32	$.63
7	$10,000	$70,000		$.64	$1.27
8	$10,000	$80,000		$1.28	$2.55
9	$10,000	$90,000		$2.56	$5.11
10	**$10,000**	**$100,000**		**$5.12**	**$10.23**

If you had chosen $10,000 a day, you would have earned $100,000 by the 10th day. If you had chosen the doubling penny, you would have earned only $10.23. Did you make the right choice?

Now, let's check out what happened in the next 10 days...

Day	**$ Paid**	**Total**	**$ Paid**	**Total**
11	$10,000	$110,000	$10.24	$20.47
12	$10,000	$120,000	$20.48	$40.95
13	$10,000	$130,000	$40.96	$81.91
14	$10,000	$140,000	$81.92	$163.83
15	$10,000	$150,000	$163.84	$327.67
16	$10,000	$160,000	$327.68	$655.35
17	$10,000	$170,000	$655.36	$1,310.71
18	$10,000	$180,000	$1,310.72	$2,621.43
19	$10,000	$190,000	$2,621.44	$5,242.87
20	**$10,000**	**$200,000**	**$5,242.88**	**$10,485.75**

Two-thirds of the month is gone. If you took the doubling penny, you would have made a total of over $10,000. If you had taken the $10,000 a day, you would have earned $200,000.

Only 10 days left...

Day	$ Paid	Total	$ Paid	Total
21	$10,000	$210,000	$10,485.76	$20,971.51
22	$10,000	$220,000	$20,971.52	$41,943.03
23	$10,000	$230,000	$41,943.04	$83,886.07
24	$10,000	$240,000	$83,886.08	$167,772.15
25	$10,000	$250,000	$167,772.16	$335,544.31
26	$10,000	$260,000	$335,544.32	$671,088.63
27	$10,000	$270,000	$671,088.64	$1,342,177.20
28	$10,000	$280,000	$1,342,177.20	$2,684,354.40
29	$10,000	$290,000	$2,684,354.40	$5,368,708.80
30	$10,000	$300,000	$5,368,708.80	$10,737,417.00

If you'd chosen $10,000 a day, you would have $300,000 at the end of 30 days. But if you'd chosen the doubling penny, you would have more than TEN MILLION DOLLARS!

On the last day alone you would have been paid more than $5 million!

This is the awesome power of compounding! When you double a small number, the result is still a small number...in the beginning. But as you continue doubling, the number gets bigger and bigger and bigger, and eventually you achieve massive growth in a short period of time.

Look again at the chart above. If you took $10,000 a day, by the 24th day you'd have a total of $240,000. With the doubling penny option, your total would have been only $167,772.16. However, look at the LAST FIVE DAYS of the month—in those last five days, your doubling penny daily income grows from $167,772.16 to $5,368,708.80!

Network marketing businesses grow the same way— slowly at first—but as you keep building, the compounding effect eventually creates incredible growth. With compounding dollars, the rate of growth in this example is 100% and stays the same. It is the passage of time that eventually creates the big numbers. With network marketing, your rate of growth actually accelerates because you are dealing with human beings, not dollars!

When you start your network marketing business, it is all about YOUR effort. But as you develop leaders, each of whom is working to build their organization (which is a part of your organization), it is no longer only your effort. Your team's collective efforts result in "compounded compounding." Your rate of growth accelerates and your organization increases at a faster pace.

Now, let's get back to the story...

"You both have great minds, and I'd love for you to reach your dream," dad told his daughters. "However, only one of you will make enough to not only pay for college, but all of the attendant living expenses as well. I already know who will reach that goal."

"One of you chose to be paid $10,000 a day, and I understand your decision. Most people would make the same selection. After all, $300,000 is an unheard of amount for 30 days work." Dad then turned to daughter #2 who had chosen the penny doubling option and said, "You took a chance and selected the doubling penny, choosing to give up the guaranteed amount without knowing how much you would be paid. Your decision to work without a guarantee has served you well. Now you can pay for your college tuition, books, lab fees, living expenses, and recreation, and still have a huge sum left over." Daughter #2 was overjoyed! (While she was sad that she hadn't gone with the doubling penny option, Daughter #1, always resilient, was able to pay all of her college expenses with the help of a part-time job and graduated a semester later than Daughter #2.)

Most people want a "guaranteed" salary. In network marketing, there's no guarantee. When starting up your business, it requires a lot of effort for relatively little reward, so it's common to have doubts about what you're doing. Many people give up around "day 20"—right before their business is about to explode. Don't give up!

COULD YOU DO THIS?

It takes time to grow a business (any business). Compounding and teamwork allow you to grow quickly. With the right training, tools, and support, a new distributor can bring one new team member on board every month for a year. Then you teach each new team member to do that very same thing. Let's see how your team can grow exponentially by doing this:

MONTH	YOU RECRUIT	TOTAL ORGANIZATION
1	1	2
2	1	4
3	1	8
4	1	16
5	1	32
6	1	64
7	1	128
8	1	256
9	1	512
10	1	1,024
11	1	2,048
12	1	4,096

In one year, by personally adding JUST ONE NEW TEAM MEMBER EACH MONTH and teaching that new member how to add one person each month, your team would grow to more than 4,000 associates! Imagine what would happen if some of your team brings in more than 12 new members in a year! And what if some of them continue to bring in new people after the first year? That means greater growth and compounding—which translates into more income and faster progress toward your financial dreams and goals!

In the first six months of your business, your organization may still be relatively small. However, check out the next six months. That's when you'll really see the results of your efforts.

Of course, it will not happen exactly like this example. Some team members will do virtually nothing. Some will add less than one new person per month to the business. Some will grow your team similar to the above example.

And a few will add many, many more than one per month (remember the concept of the four aces?) These few will bring thousands of team members into your business and build your fortune. This is the miracle of network marketing!

Acknowledgments

JUDY O'HIGGINS

To my partners, lifelong friends and co-authors Kristi Lee and Karen Palmer—thank you for embracing my dream. Thank you for joining me in finding a way to encourage and empower women to change their lives and get free through network marketing. Thank you for believing in my vision and for all the brilliance you brought to this book. Enrolling you in my mission was the best thing I could have done! I am a better person for knowing you, and for all you have contributed to *License to Dream* and to my life. It has been my great honor to work with you both and the best is yet to come!

To John for your patience with all the hours spent on this project, for your continued support and for believing in me all the way. I love you and will always be grateful for having you in my life—I am blessed!

To my team who also believe in me, encourage and inspire me every day to be my best and build our business with trust and integrity. You are all like family to me and I cherish the relationships we share. There are too many to name them all (over 5,300 as of this writing) but special thanks to Dawn, Kathy, Jules, Bridget, Frank, local team members Geri, Susan, Carolanne, Carolyn, Sharon, Stu, Julie, Gwendolyn, Leslie, Kathy and Sandy.

Very special thanks to Debbie B. for your unwavering encouragement and for always supporting me and my goals. Special thanks to Julie for your friendship, caring, and for cheering on my progress as this endeavor became a reality.

To Jordan for your amazing knowledge, training, leadership, and mostly for your gift of keeping it simple so that I always believed I could do it. You changed my life.

Finally to all women network marketers—your courage to dare to be different and not settle for what society considers "normal" inspires me every day. Thank you for those who came before to pave the way, to those who are now navigating the journey to financial freedom, and to those who may be inspired to take their first steps because of this book. Keep the faith and don't quit until you reach your destination—freedom!

KRISTI LEE

Thank you to my dear friend, Judy O'Higgins, who invited me into her dream of helping women all over the world. It has been an honor to be on this journey with you and Karen Palmer. We are just getting started in changing the world, one person at a time. You have given me one of the best gifts I could have—your friendship. Thank you for believing in me, for your support, and traveling the world together—you have changed my life forever!

Thank you to my mom—your unwavering belief in me and your tireless support has made it possible for me to inspire people all over the world. I love you! To my daughter Jade, for inspiring me every day to wake up with excitement to what our future looks like (and being coachable when I teach you how to be your own boss!)

Thank you to Kody and Jodi Bateman for having the courage to persevere and to lead with your hearts; you have created a company culture that is world-class. Thank you to Jordan Adler for being unshakeable in your leadership and mentoring me with visionary wisdom. Thank you to my team, many of you who have become lifelong friends, for allowing me to lead and giving me grace when I make mistakes! To my cousin, Nina Ten, thank you for living life with passion and bringing your positive energy to every person you meet. To Carrie Cole, you are one of the most courageous women I know. To Glen and Carla Forthun, thank you for being great friends and sharing your lives with me. To Tracy Burns and Ramona Syburg, thank you for believing in the gifts we have been blessed with and having faith we can make a difference.

Thank you to Eric Lofholm for teaching me skills that will serve my team and me for a lifetime and to Tom "Big Al" Schreiter for being willing to share your knowledge selflessly. A special thank you to the leaders in our industry, who have and will unselfishly teach me your skills so I can pay it forward to future generations, I appreciate you letting me stand on your shoulders!

A special thank you to Jim and Leslee Testa for letting us use your beautiful car for our cover photo—we are grateful for your trust and faith in our vision for this project!

KAREN PALMER

To Judy, thank you for inviting me to be a part of your vision of sharing network marketing with women. I'm so thankful and blessed to have been able to work on this project with you and Kristi. You started out as my mentors and business partners, but you have become wonderful, lifelong friends along the way. Judy, you are an inspiration to me and to everyone on your team. Thank you for believing in me.

To my husband, Ryan, and kids, Megan, Tristan, & Josyan, thank you for supporting me as I spent countless hours working on this project. You are my biggest *why*. I love you all so much, and I wouldn't be here without you. Thank you for dreaming big with me!

Thank you to my mom and dad for always teaching me to do my best, no matter what. You instilled in me the values of hard work, commitment, and discipline and taught me to believe in myself. Dad, I wish you were here to see this, but I know you're cheering me on. You always believed I could do anything. And to my stepdad Rod, thank you for believing in me and becoming an indispensible part of our family. I am so blessed to have such a tightly knit family—you may not always agree with me or "get" me, but you love me anyway and cheer me on. Thank you!

To my wonderful mother-in-law, Kathy—thank you for not giving up on me and persisting until you finally "signed me up." How great is it to have a family –in-law that loves me like their own and supports me. Thank you to you and Gary for raising incredible sons—especially the one I'm blessed to be married to.

To the amazing CEO and the phenomenal leaders in my company, who inspired me to catch the vision and dream big. Because of your coaching, I dug my heels in and made a choice to succeed. To leaders everywhere—remember that your words not only inspire people in the moment—but for a lifetime. My expanding vision has led me to places I'd never dreamed of. Thank you for being willing to take the time to share your wisdom and belief with me and everyone else out there on this road to freedom.

Last, but certainly not least, to my Heavenly Father. Thank you for creating me in Your image—for having a plan for my life—for creating good things for me to accomplish before I was even born. Thank you for giving me the desires of my heart and the courage to believe they were possible.

About the authors

Judy O'Higgins was raised in Connecticut, but made her way west after graduating from the University of Michigan School of Social Work with an MSW and serving for two years in VISTA (the domestic Peace Corps) in the 60s. She lived in San Diego for many years, but migrated to Arizona to become a homeowner with land, a garden, and various animals, including chickens, goats, a horse, dogs, and a cat.

Judy ran a 30-day to recovery program for substance abusers in Sedona, Ariz., for four years. That was her last job working for someone else. In 1990, she opened a private counseling practice and became a solopreneur, helping hundreds of women to overcome negative programming and empower themselves to better relationships, jobs, self-esteem, and family functionality. Her greatest love was helping women to believe in themselves and to do things they didn't think were possible.

Judy was introduced to network marketing in 1996 and instantly loved the concept of working with teams in a "win-win" environment for the common goal of financial freedom. Her first company failed, temporarily ending Judy's dream of retiring with residual income for life. Now she knows that was just practice for her second company, where she has risen to be in the top 25 distributors and created enough monthly residual income to retire from her counseling career after just two years.

Judy is still helping to empower women to a better life by believing in themselves and doing things they didn't think were possible—getting their dreams back and creating financial freedom for themselves and their families through network marketing. Her goals include national and worldwide travel as her company expands internationally to spread the concept of residual income through network marketing to women worldwide. She encourages every woman to dream big, work hard, and see the job through to the reward of freedom and a family legacy of generational wealth.

Kristi Lee was born and raised in Los Angeles, California, the youngest of three girls in a second generation Chinese family. Kristi was taught growing up that success meant graduating college and getting a good paying job. She graduated college with a Bachelor of Science degree in business administration and worked in the corporate world in marketing and retail for 20 years. Her responsibilities included category management (sales growth and advertising for health and beauty products for 2,300 retail stores across the U.S.).

Kristi's corporate career involved multiple moves to different states and 4½ years ago was again told she was going to be moved, this time to Boise, Idaho. She had a feeling the company was not making the move for the right reasons, and walked away from her 20-year career. Seven months later, after most of her colleagues had taken the move, the company announced it was for sale, stranding many of her friends in Boise where the job market was not robust and now the housing market was going to see a flood of "for sale" signs. It was then that she realized she never wanted to work for a company where she had a boss and vowed she would help as many people have choices about being free—from job stress, financial debt, and too much time away from their families.

Her first experience with network marketing was negative, when she was a young child and family members on her father's side were involved in a company that would never reveal their name until they tricked you into attending one of their opportunity meetings. Kristi was re-introduced to network marketing in 2006, while going through a divorce and having her corporate job move out of state. Once she fell in love with her company's product and service, and the idea of leveraging time, she left the corporate world behind and has never looked back.

Kristi is enjoying raising her daughter, Jade, and traveling the world while building her business. She has a passion for inspiring women and children to step into their power and share their gifts and talents with the world.

Born and raised in Arizona, **Karen Palmer** grew up in the small town of Camp Verde where she grew to love the slow and quiet country life. In 1995, Karen left Camp Verde to attend college, marrying her high-school sweetheart Ryan in 1996. After graduating from Northern Arizona University with a BA in English in 1998 and a MA in Rhetoric in 2000, Karen and Ryan moved to Phoenix, where Karen taught composition full-time for two years at Grand Canyon University.

In 2002 their first child, a beautiful baby girl, was born. Desiring to raise their children in the small town atmosphere they loved, the Palmers moved back to Camp Verde, where Ryan began a thriving contracting business building custom homes. Over the next few years, Ryan and Karen added two handsome boys to their young family. Karen's heart's desire has always been to be home with her children, and she believes that being a mom is one of the most meaningful titles a woman can hold.

However, in 2008, Karen saw her life of being a stay-at-home mom jeopardized by the failing economy. Together with her husband Ryan, Karen decided to take a leap of faith and begin building a network marketing business that would enable her to stay home with her kids and protect their family from the market downturn.

For Karen, network marketing is a source of hope in these trying times, not only for herself, but for many other families looking for financial security and freedom. In building her business, Karen learned to dream big, and is now focused on helping other women like herself achieve financial freedom through network marketing. Her passion is to help women find balance between pursuing their passions and being present in their homes.

License to Dream is also available as an eBook.
Visit www.eagleonepublishing.com for details.

EAGLE ONE

PUBLISHING

Salt Lake City, Utah